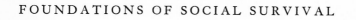
FOUNDATIONS OF SOCIAL SURVIVAL

RELIGION IS POLITICS,
AND POLITICS IS BROTHERHOOD

William Blake

FOUNDATIONS OF
Social Survival

by JOHN LINDBERG

NEW YORK 1953
COLUMBIA UNIVERSITY PRESS

THE ROCKEFELLER FOUNDATION

HAS GENEROUSLY PROVIDED FUNDS

TO MEET PART OF THE COST

OF PREPARATION AND PUBLICATION

OF THIS WORK

LIBRARY OF CONGRESS CATALOG CARD NUMBER: 53-11452

COPYRIGHT, 1953, COLUMBIA UNIVERSITY PRESS, NEW YORK
PUBLISHED IN GREAT BRITAIN, CANADA, INDIA, AND PAKISTAN
BY GEOFFREY CUMBERLEGE, OXFORD UNIVERSITY PRESS
LONDON, TORONTO, BOMBAY, AND KARACHI
MANUFACTURED IN THE UNITED STATES OF AMERICA

ACKNOWLEDGMENTS

THE WRITING of this work was made possible by a membership at the Institute for Advanced Study and a special grant from the Rockefeller Foundation, which has also contributed to the publication of the book.

I would try, in vain, to express my deep debt of gratitude to the group of social scientists working at the Institute. Nor can I thank appropriately all those who have read the manuscript in part or in whole. Indeed, I owe so much to the affection, encouragement, and often severe criticisms of my friends that I have come to feel that this volume represents as much the expression of certain common attitudes and aspirations as it does one individual's contribution to the tradition.

Dr. Paul Clement has been a most sensitive editor; I am indebted to him also for careful checking and for an occasional translation in the quotations from Greek and Latin authors.

JOHN LINDBERG

Institute for Advanced Study
Princeton, New Jersey

CONTENTS

PART I

The City as Reason

FOR [MAN] SHOULD PERSEVERE UNTIL HE HAS
ACHIEVED ONE OF TWO THINGS; EITHER HE SHOULD
DISCOVER, OR BE TAUGHT THE TRUTH . . . OR, IF
THIS BE IMPOSSIBLE, I WOULD HAVE HIM TAKE THE
BEST AND MOST IRREFRAGABLE OF HUMAN THEORIES,
AND LET THIS BE THE RAFT UPON WHICH HE SAILS
THROUGH LIFE—NOT WITHOUT RISK, AS I ADMIT, IF
HE CANNOT FIND SOME WORD OF GOD WHICH WILL
MORE SURELY AND SAFELY CARRY HIM.—*Plato*

I

The Founding

OF THE CITY

COME, THEN, LET US CREATE A CITY FROM THE
BEGINNING, IN OUR THEORY. ITS REAL CREATOR, AS
IT APPEARS, WILL BE OUR NEEDS.—*Plato* [1]

MAN MODIFIES ENVIRONMENT and environment man; social theory,
therefore cannot afford to build on postulates which define either
man or nature as changeless entities. In that case it would have to
rebuild its structure each time there happened to occur some
change in the concepts supplied either by psychology or by the
natural sciences. Social theory is soundly founded only as long as
it, from social observation, postulates in man and nature such
characters as will account for relevant social events in the simplest
manner compatible with logical consistency.

Now, experience informs us that there exist some apparently
lasting *relationships* between man and nature. They express themselves as "natural wants," and can be met variously; but if they
are not met, man cannot survive. He needs food and other necessaries of life; he must produce. He is mortal; he must reproduce.
He has enemies; he must defend himself. The conditions dictated
by nature to man as a species carry over to society; any lasting
grouping of men must provide sustenance for its members, as well

[1] *Republic,* 369c.

as reproduce and defend itself. And in this sense, it is natural to visualize society as a sequence of human events arranging themselves in patterns to meet these primary *social functions*.

But if nature is niggard, if man's productive and combative powers are limited, resources required to meet the social functions become scarce, the functions compete among themselves. Too much or too little cannot be given to any one without causing a destructive disequilibrium. We are justified in saying then that social survival requires a balance between the social functions. If this balance were the gift of God, Nature, or Evolution, risk of social disintegration could not exist; but the death of societies is the commonplace of history. The maintenance of balance requires some effort, for, though the framework of government changes and appears occasionally to result from the operation of semi-automatic mechanisms, the creation and maintenance of these arrangements always requires an effort which (like all social functions) uses up resources and energies necessarily drawn from society's common pool. Since the maintenance of balance presupposes the existence of order, it seems logical to consider order as a fourth social function to be added to production, reproduction, and defense.

In a first definition the problem of social survival consists, then, in striking the right balance between the several social functions. Social theory should account for how such balance is achieved, maintained, and dissolved. In order to throw light on problems of this kind, reason suggests no better method than the construction of theoretical models. Indeed, while this method is generally ascribed to natural science, it was first used by social philosophers; social models have long been known under the name of *cities*. Like all theoretical models, the city is constructed for a definite purpose;

it tries meaningfully to arrange and interpret phenomena given in experience. Its validity is not primarily a matter of supporting illustration and concrete detail, but it has to be modified or abandoned if opposed by a single discordant fact. The city represents a conscious theoretical abstraction, and it grows more abstract the more heterogeneous the mass of data with which it has to cope.

It would be possible to construct a city from the beginning; but it is preferable to use terms which are integral parts of tradition, for theory and practice are interdependent. It is true that practice may antedate theory, and that social life is more ancient than social theory. But as it is unlikely that the automobile could have appeared prior to a body of systematic knowledge of mechanics, so it is unlikely that complex and highly integrated societies could have arisen prior to thought based upon a body of systematic knowledge of society, even if such theory may have been forgotten or from the beginning hidden from public view. Positive theory should render previous theory explicit, for observation and theory are themselves social forces, and thus data relevant for social study; the more evolved societies become, the more important is previous theory in explaining actual developments. Interpreting experience, then, rather than charting the boundless land of potentiality, social theory must find the means of including previous theory among its own data, and so on in a self-perpetuating series in which social theory becomes itself the partial but necessary object of its own study. How this introspection affects the total body of theory will become apparent at certain points of the argument.

We are fortunate that we possess in Plato's *Republic* a city which is perhaps the archetype of all theoretical models. It consciously aims at representing, not reality directly, but conditions required to be met in a surviving state. For those philosophers who aim at

founding a city, Plato says, "will take a real city and the habits of
its people, as they might a tablet, and first wipe it clean . . . They
would refuse to take in hand individual or city, or to legislate,
before they either received a clean slate or themselves made it
clean." [2] And having eliminated from experience what is accidental to their purpose, "they would sketch the figure of the constitution . . . would glance frequently in either direction, at
justice, beauty, sobriety and the like as they are in the nature of
things, and alternately at that which they were trying to reproduce in mankind, mingling and blending from various pursuits
that hue of the flesh which Homer too called the image and likeness of God." [3]

As the purpose of the *Republic* is to elucidate the nature of
justice, we must ask what is meant there by justice. It is, Plato says,
"the power of each individual [or group of individuals] to do his
own work" [4] in the interest of the whole. It is seen that the Platonic
meaning of justice is essentially one of social balance. It is not the
task of the social theorist to decide from the outset whether or not
the conditions required for perfect balance are ever likely to be
realized in actual life, and thus to determine by a priori dictum
whether or not enduring social life is possible. "We are inquiring
into the nature of absolute justice . . . and injustice. . . . We
[are] to look at these in order that we may judge of our own happiness and unhappiness according to the standard which they exhibit and the degree in which we resemble them, *but not with any
view of showing that they could exist in fact.*" [5] This should dispose
of the utopian interpretation of the *Republic;* and it would serve
no purpose to concern ourselves in this study with the web of
scholarship spun around Platonic thought. Free of any ambition

[2] *Republic,* 501a.   [3] *Ibid.,* 501a-b.   [4] *Ibid.,* 433d.   [5] *Ibid.,* 472c-d.

to find out what Plato "really" meant or to compass the whole of his thought, we turn to him directly and adopt from him such concepts as happen to be needed for our own gropings after light upon the lasting problems of social life.

In founding a city, or social model, we are at liberty to begin almost where we please; for the social process is seamlessly one, and sooner or later we shall cover it all. But as man's dependence upon nature gives rise to the first social functions, it seems expedient to consider with Plato how social events can be shaped to meet them. Considering man's "natural wants" he distinguishes between the four social functions, and divides the citizens into four groups or classes, each representing one function:

1. The *Guardians* (or magistrates), representing the function of order.
2. The *Auxiliaries* (or soldiers), representing the function of defense.
3. The *Productive Class* (merchants, artisans, farmers, slaves, etc.), representing the function of production.
4. The *Community of Women and Children* (or families), representing the function of reproduction.

Whether or not we choose to attribute each function to a particular class would, as yet, seem mainly a question of analytical convenience. Even Plato ran against difficulties in maintaining a strict separation. This difficulty is, of course, most acute in the case of the community of women and children. His method of analysis would demand a clear separation of the reproductive function from the others; but at least in this case he realized that a certain overlapping was inevitable. He speaks with some unease and in the end he may have left the majority in possession of some kind of normal family life. In the first approach we shall disregard this complication and proceed on the assumption that society can achieve a full functional classification.

Next, man's dependence upon nature requires that a city should possess some natural resources, a specific natural environment, and certain skills of the people in utilizing them. When Plato built the Republic he had in mind—not the wide expanse of the Barbarian world—but the highly evolved city-states of Hellas. He derived his concepts from his own culture, but even if he had lived at some other time or place, he could still have accomplished his purpose. He could have adopted social habits to fit many kinds of natural circumstance and technical knowledge. For as in the art of ship-building there are principles that apply to the construction of all ships, so in the art of city-building there are principles that apply to all cities regardless of most natural and technical differences. But Plato conceived his city in terms of natural environment and habits lifted from—or implicit in—a Hellenic environment. The ways of doing things, or habits, he had in mind were political, re-lating to the ways of government and administration; they were military, relating to the ways of war; they were reproductive, relat-ing to the ways of breeding and rearing of children; they were religious, relating to the educational and moral aspects of the city. These several systems of habits are naturally not identical with that state of technical or other knowledge supposed to exist at a given time or place. They are actual ways of doing things, sequences of events which, while perhaps contained in an abstract body of knowledge as potentiality and alternative, become socially opera-tive only under conditions determined by the system as a whole. The more the body of abstract knowledge happens to increase, the greater becomes the variety of potential habit; but there is no reason why abstract knowledge and actual habit should not fluctuate independently of each other. It seems likely, for instance, that the sum of abstract knowledge, if such summation be permissible, reaches a maximum at the ends of civilizations when the efficiency of actual habit is already decreasing. Similarly, in spite of an almost common body of knowledge, different countries show even now great differences as to efficiency of habit.

But it is premature to consider these problems belonging to the complex of questions raised by social change. We may here adopt almost any system of operative social habit; we can build the city in many climates, at different levels of skill and natural resources. It is important to remember only that once we have had our wish in all these respects, we cannot change our mind. For in order to study change in habit, we must first learn more about habit in general. And for the same reason we must, to start with, consider a closed system. Defense was included among the primary social functions; but it establishes relations between several cities and opens the gate through which outside impulse can enter into the closed system. In the first analysis it is expedient, therefore, to give the defense function a value of zero (or any low constant value).

Hence, imagine that we have determined, not without arbitrariness, man's need for food, shelter, and the modest comforts of life; that we have endowed the city with natural resources adequate to its needs; that we have let it adopt an initial state of integrated habit suited to its situation. By theoretical fiat we have re-created a situation which in reality would have emerged out of a long historical process. The art of government would essentially seem then to consist in inducing man to follow the habit dictated by the necessities of this system as a whole.

Plato was not greatly concerned in the details of habit; he introduces the famous, but little understood, device of a perfect ruler.

Placing at the helm of the Republic a philosopher who personifies social justice, or social balance, Plato is freed from tedious detail. He was not naive enough to believe it likely that a perfect ruler could be found; and still less a whole succession of them. And if we find it expedient to grant Plato his sweeping assumption in the first analysis, it is for a reason. The perfect ruler is not a phantom created by wishful thinking of an unpractical philosopher, but an analytical device (corresponding to the scientists' "initial state") which permits us to perceive and analyze phenomena, pertaining to rule, which require simultaneous recognition with habit in the construction of the city.

The stream of events led in the channels of social balance represent the patterns of social survival. In other words, social habit represents the forms in which the "human copy" has to fit. But, if so, is man either capable or willing to be molded in the forms of perfection? No a priori answer is likely to be true, and founders of states must proceed experimentally and "mingle and temper the various elements of life into the image of a man. . . . One feature they will erase and another they will put in, until they have made the ways of men, within the limits of the possible, agreeable and dear to the ways of God." [6] It is necessary to consider how men respond to the pressure of social habit; but in order to do this, consider first the general type of social structure that has begun to emerge out of Platonic thought.

By entrusting each social function to a special group or class, the city is formed vertically into a hierarchical pyramid. The necessity of this construction becomes easy to understand if it is recalled that the function of order—and with it the responsibility of leading the flow of events in patterns capable of survival—belongs to the

[6] *Republic,* 501b-c.

ruler. The state must then be so constructed that each class, and each subject within each class, performs the task given to it in accordance with the ruler's will which, by definition, personifies social justice or balance. The city's order may be likened to that which a gardener imposes on nature. The pattern-forming force resides in the gardener: if he tires in his efforts, the garden in time reverts to nature. Similarly, if the ruler tires in his efforts, the city will in time dissolve into its elements. A gardener must overcome the resistance of nature to the pattern imposed; and unless the ruler meets spontaneous submission to his will, he has to overcome a resistance in human nature to the pattern he tries to impose. And in this vertical construction of society, the highest virtue of the subjects becomes obedience to the ruler's will; authority emanating from above represents the objectively given conditions of common survival. Before, then, we can profitably discuss the details of the system of habit, it is necessary to see how men react to any habit-system imposed upon them.

A social pattern represents a stream of events; and these events are either themselves energy or expressions of energy. The existence of such a social energy is a legitimate inference from social observation; and unless this energy is conceived as flowing into society from some outside source, it must be assumed to originate in man. It does not greatly matter how we describe this energy, or bundle of energies—instinct, passion, appetite, emotion, urges, drives, etc. —as long as we understand under these names the energy that is expressed in social action. And whatever the ultimate character of this energy, or energies, they are malleable into many forms of behavior. They can be and are led into streams of events serving the function of production: one may speak about an alimentary or economic instinct. They can be and are led into streams of events

serving the reproductive function: one may speak about an erotic or
parental instinct. They can be and are led into streams of events
serving the defense function: one may speak about a combative
instinct. They can be and are led into streams of events serving
the order function: one may speak about an instinct of combination
(or reason). Observation may add to the list of such apparent in-
stincts and indeed they are variously described and catalogued by
the contending schools of psychology. Each such construct may be
used in the creation of theories reflecting aspects of reality. But
it is precisely against such partial theory that we have to guard
here. Man is one—the economic man, the erotic man, the combative
man, and the rational man must all be accounted for in general
theory. These primary energies are on the whole directed and
distributed in such a way as to permit individual survival. In a
general way, therefore, Plato accepts and further develops the
Democritean idea of man himself being a *mikros kosmos.*

But observation has taught us that the individual does not, without some friction and resistance, mold his individual behavior
according to the social dictates of order. To account for these resistances—separating the human society from such societies as
that of the beehive—we infer in man a further force which we call
private reason or intelligence. There is nothing to prevent the social theorist from conceiving this force as an aspect of instinct, but
it is more convenient to give it independent status. We define intelligence as that force or faculty which seems to compel men to
seek consistency between premise and conclusion, between ends
and means, between habit and belief. Hence, in both man and society the rational principle is of one and the same nature: private
reason looks for realization of ends implicit in instinct; social
reason for social survival. And it is exactly for that reason that they

are bound to collide. The ruler, personifying social reason, asks men to give up the pursuit of such ends and the exercise of such faculties as are incompatible with their station as subjects. He asks them to perform their appointed task well. And as social reason is the monopoly of the ruler, the requirements of social reason will appear to the individual irrational. The subject is to be deprived not only of liberty of action but also of a meaningful explanation of the behavior imposed upon him. As society evolves it bestows benefits on all; it may greatly ease individual struggle for survival; it creates, in fact, such values and such characters as we have come to consider truly human. But however benevolent rule may appear, it imposes restraints upon human nature. The rational state tends to be followed like a shadow by a feeling of irrationality; it seems to deprive men of the possibility of living, even if tragically, in ways meaningful to themselves. Speaking as ruler, reason can offer men no valid explanation why they should become the instruments of another's will.

The forceful, and apparently arbitrary, suppression of individual ends, tends to create certain reactions. In proportion to the social pressure one observes individual reactions meaningfully contained in the concept of frustration. Arbitrary rule—or more precisely, what must appear as arbitrary rule—violates the subject's feeling of private rationality and creates feelings of resentment, anger, and hate, which focus themselves on the ruler and the symbols of order. The many private frustrations combine into larger patterns which render rule difficult, unpleasant, and, after a point, impossible. Hence, if rule (and thus social survival) is not to become impossible, there must be found some means of containing such anti-patterns within tolerable limits.

The reaction of private reason to rule becomes in the ruler's mind

a testimony to the depravity of human nature itself. Rulers seem to
have acted on the assumption that subjects can be made obedient
only if compelled by fear. The variety and refinement of physical
and psychological sanctions that have been invented and used are
truly astounding. Fear has become so common a reaction to rule
that it seems almost excusable for a ruler to fall into the habit of
nourishing the idea that fear alone is a sufficient instrument of
rule.

But while force and fear may be necessary instruments of rule, it
does not follow that they are sufficient instruments. Social theory
cannot neglect the reactions to these instruments; we noted that
the frustrations they create in individuals tend to combine in social
antipatterns. The fears and hates which grow up between subjects
and rulers are cumulative and they become mutual. They may
lead to destructive outbreaks of violence; but even if such outbreaks
are avoided, the danger of outbreaks, implicit in fear and frustration, impels the ruler to transfer more and more resources and
energies to the physical arm of the function of order. But as societies' resources are limited, such transfers begin after a point to
starve other necessary social functions and lead to destructive social
unbalance. Hence, social survival demands some kind of arrangement that prevents the runaway expansion of the function of order.

Having raised this question we become aware of the orderly
progression of Plato's thought. For it would be pointless to discuss
the details of right habit if human nature should oppose insur-
mountable barriers to any imposed order. And if the function of
order remains unbounded, no lasting social life is at all possible.
The inquiry into justice would be little more than an exercise of
thought. Experience itself of course contradicts these extreme conclusions. Societies have existed for quite long periods of time, and

in order to understand how this is possible we have to inquire into how the function of order is actually bounded.

". . . When the reasoning and human and ruling power is asleep, the monster within us, gorged with meat or drink, starts up and having shaken off sleep, goes forth to satisfy his desires; and there is no conceivable folly or crime which at such a time, when he has parted company with all shame or sense, he is not ready to commit: he does not shrink from attempting to have intercourse with his mother in fancy or with anyone else, man, god, or monster; he is ready for any foul murder; he abstains from no food, and, in a word, falls short of no extreme of folly and depravity." [7] This is the monster conceived in the shadow of man's frustrated appetite. Rule necessarily nurtures him, and in his proper time he is born —with violence—to the city. To forestall this dread thing, the ruler must try to minimize, if not eliminate, the conflict between private and social reason: he must at least assure himself of some voluntary assent to rule.

[7] *Ibid.*, 571c-d.

2

The Gods

OF THE CITY

HOW YOUR WORDS SEEM TO HESITATE ON
YOUR LIPS!
YOU WILL NOT WONDER, I REPLIED, AT MY
HESITATION WHEN YOU HAVE HEARD.—*Plato* [1]

MAN LIVES IN SOCIETY and his behavior is conditioned by his natural and social environment, or what is usually thought of as
"reality." But, in the subjective sense, decisions leading to action
are conditioned, not directly by reality, but by the reflection of it in
the mind. Men form certain ideas or notions about their environment; some are plain, concrete, and fairly accurate; others are
complex, abstract, and approximate; some, finally, seem to have no
foundation whatsoever in reality. Still everything seems to indi-
cate that the rationality of the common run of men is satisfied as
long as there is what they consider an agreement between premise
and conclusion. If they believe that the earth is flat, they will shape
their actions accordingly; they will not set out trying to discover
a western route to the Indies, even if they otherwise should happen
to have the means and incentive to do so.

Imagine, then, that for reasons of state, a ruler desires to prevent his subjects from undertaking voyages of discovery. He may

[1] *Republic,* 414c.

pass a law prohibiting them; he may police his ports and prevent his subjects from building ships capable of long voyages. But such a course involves expenditure of force, and it creates discontent and frustration among the adventurers. This frustration would be dangerous in proportion to the individual impulse for action; and a wise ruler would try to have his way and create the desired useful habit without waste of physical force, and without arousing opposition against himself. Indeed, would he not tell his subjects that the earth is flat? For if they were to believe this fiction (and not expose it to experimental verification), they would not dream of undertaking expeditions which to them would seem as patently absurd as voyages to the moon. Their inaction would not seem imposed upon them by the will of another man but as an intelligent adaptation to the general conditions of life. "And while people hate *men* who oppose their impulses, even if they oppose them rightly," [2] they seem rather to pride themselves on being able to respond rationally to what, to them, appears as natural necessity. Hence, by projecting suitable ideas into the minds of men, the ruler apparently has a means of decreasing, or dissolving, the conflict between himself and his subjects. By the wise and systematic use of such projections ("needful falsehoods," fictions, or myths) he may forestall the birth of monsters. He can make ruling much safer and much more pleasant.

It may be objected that the telling of lies is unworthy of a good ruler; that it is indicative of deceit and cunning rather than of statecraft. But says Plato, "Such . . . are our principles of theology—some tales are to be told, and others are not to be told to our disciples from their youth upwards." [3] And of such stuff does Plato create a secondary system of government and, indeed, found

[2] Aristotle, *Nicomachean Ethics,* 1180a (Ross).   [3] Plato, *op. cit.,* 386a.

a science. Historical myths are of a wide variety, but myths, to
become socially relevant or operative as projections, are not arbitrary fancies but stand in determinate relations, discoverable by
analysis, to the social situation as a whole. Projections can be observed in all human societies and are data relevant to social ex-
periences; they demand as such their rightful place in social theory itself. They cannot be dismissed by private disapproval, or
exiled to the intellectually barren land of superstition; and, before
we press on into the country of myth and consider the principles
of their formation, a few words of warning are in place.

Like Plato we find it expedient to study myth from the viewpoint of the ruler. This may cause some misunderstanding among
the literal-minded; but as they, in any event, are likely to feel
disconcerted in the subtle and perhaps cynical company of mythmakers, it may suffice to point out that the ruler here represents
only a theoretical device, permitting us to deal conveniently with
the complex of social necessity. It is not to be thought that myths
are actually invented and thought out by personal rulers; and
Plato, as he shows himself in the *Laws,* is aware of the long historical process out of which myths have probably emerged. Like
him we deal here not with all myths but only with myths attached to a system of particular social habits.

Secondly, social theory does not consider myths under the restricted aspect of individual psychology. No doubt myths spring
up in response to many different stimuli. It seems altogether plau-
sible that they can be interpreted, among other things, in terms of
individual compensation mechanisms serving to cover up a too
harsh social reality; it would be surprising if they could not be
explained in terms of rationalizations of private or class interest.
And why should not some groups be more fertile in myth inven-

tion than others, or more skillful in imposing them as projections on society? However this may be, socially operative myths emerge upon the public plane through a long process of trial, error, and competition; they have had to pass the test of social fitness and can be studied, therefore, in terms of social survival and by means of functional analysis.

Thirdly, the origin of myth is likely to be forgotten. In real cities, all, or almost all, inhabitants are likely to have lost consciousness of their nature. It may, for this reason, be permissible to point out that the usefulness of social projections bears no relation to their truth in the sense of natural science. Projections are themselves social data (however true or false in respect to the relationships they pretend to represent); it is quite another matter that their content, in order that myths should become and remain operative, should appear probably true, or at any rate, uncontroverted by common experience. Potency of myths depends upon—not that they should be fact, but that they should appear as fact. Minds trained from infancy in the belief in certain projections can hardly be expected to distinguish between everyday facts and social projections masquerading as facts. Subjects (as opposed to rulers) must be trained to tell the truth, Plato teaches. But subjects would almost automatically denounce a projection if they came to suspect that it did not represent a "fact," in the ordinary sense. And such is the hold of illusion and habit that even mature students of society fall into the same error and advance upon the exposed myths like Don Quixote charging the windmills: but founders of states could not have reached eminence ignorant of the nature and functions of myth. Such knowledge is implicit also in the popular notion that religion is needed to keep the state together and prevent unrest among the people.

Returning to the main theme, recall that the ruler has already developed an initial system of habit which meets the objective conditions of social balance. His task is next to develop and impose a system of projections (or socially operative myths) united to this construct. The social habits can be conceived in innumerable forms, which in varying combinations can be made to meet the requirements of balance. And as habits change, the system of projection has to be changed too. A system of projections suited to guard one particular balance is *ipso facto* unsuited to guard another. Social projections become functions of the system of habit as a whole; no projection system, therefore, can be universally applicable *in toto*. In other words, it can be said that a universal and unchangeable system of projections would also imply a universal and unchangeable set of social habits. Hence, in the Platonic construct of the city it becomes obvious and incontroversial that the social "ideal is nothing else than the material world reflected by the human mind, and translated into forms of thought." [4] All founders of actual states have proceeded on what should be a fairly obvious insight.

A sysem of projections is composed of myths supporting particular habits; to a totality of habit there will correspond a totality of myth. Both systems should be consistent and, superimposed, should form a unity. But as we have every reason to suspect that myths may tend to spring up in many places, the ruler has the further task of keeping order in the field of beliefs. Some myths may be socially irrelevant, and be dismissed as pure works of art or superstition; some myths may be harmful to established habits. As such myths, however loosely, are joined to a system of projection, they tend to affect society; myths are good

[4] Karl Marx, *Capital* (The Modern Library, New York, 1906), p. 25.

servants but bad masters, and the ruler must concern himself with myth-formation no less than with habit-formation. With an eye to the given system of habit, he must establish order in the fields of worship, religion, philosophy, education, art, etc. He must limit the freedom of expression, and if possible, thought; for it would hardly be reasonable to entrust the protection of the social balance to the ruler, and at the same time withhold the means necessary to this end. In the following we assume that the rulers have the means of such inner control. It is true that myths are meaningful in several contexts; but we consider them here only under the social aspect.

To each city—and to each particular position of its balance in time—there corresponds, then, one system (or possibly several alternative systems) of projections which, if generally accepted as fact, would dissolve the conflict between social and individual reason. The system of projection becomes more complex, and possibly more subtle, as the city evolves, but such evolution does not decrease the necessity of myth. It should be understood that social evolution affects the particular form and complexity of myth, not its necessity. Indeed, a given function may be met by several alternative means; pillars in a temple, for instance, serve their function of supporting the ceiling, though they are made of different materials, formed in several shapes, and painted in many colors. Similarly a system of habit can be rationalized in many ways and decorated by fancy to take on many deceptive shapes and colors. In the analysis of myth it is important, therefore, to separate the objectively given function, or content, and the accidental, more or less arbitrary form. A philosopher can, from a given system of myth, fairly accurately divine the corresponding system of habit; he is much less able to divine, from a given system of habit, the form of the corresponding myth system—even though he would probably not go far wrong in predicting its myth-content.

The essential relationship between the systems of habit and myth might perhaps be made clearer by means of a figure. Imagine the subjects of a city as spectators regarding a picture on the wall. The picture represents the objectively given system of habit: it appears to each beholder, harsh and meaningless. The ruler now gives each subject a pair of spectacles; but the glasses have etched upon them a pattern of myth. When the subject views the picture, the pattern of the picture and the pattern on the glasses fall into a common pattern. And if the glasses are skillfully made, the illusion of one real pattern becomes perfect. The social habit-pattern becomes meaningful and rational in the terms of each individual. And if the subjects from now on are induced to wear the glasses, they will forget the original pattern of habit, and believe that the combined pattern (being the more meaningful) is also the "real" pattern.

The pattern of myth etched upon the social spectacles represents the city in an inner form, reflecting its inner necessities. The projections have a real existence only in the private mind, but, since they are necessary for organized social life, they may be conceived as representing the city in an inner form; and as we may summarize the system of habit under the name of the *outer kingdom,* so we may summarize the system of myth under the name of the *inner kingdom.* Hence, there is nothing of what is popularly understood as mysticism in the concept of the inner kingdom; it deals only with the universally observed phenomena of myth which, as much as those of habit, are part of social "reality." And a myth does not lose its nature of myth should it, in terms of contemporary knowledge, be considered as objectively or scientifically "true." Both habit and myth are needed to explain and analyze surviving societies; both can be analyzed in functional terms; both represent aspects of one and the same complex of interrelated phenomena.

If the picture on the wall does not change, and if the spectacles are skillfully made, the individual would lose consciousness of the existence of the two separate systems. The inner system, in particular, would become incapable of being observed, and it would be taken as part of reality in general. Such a situation—or perfect *inner balance*—represents, by definition, the point of maximum stability for the social system as a whole. But needless to say, like the outer balance, it represents a conceptual tool; perfect social balances are just as unlikely to be actually realized as the perfect equilibria of natural science.

It will be understood then why an analysis of myth-content is possible only in the terms of given systems of habit and not by a metaphysical or factual analysis of "truth" of myth. We are interested here in understanding myth in general rather than particular myths; but, for the sake of illustration, consider the outlines of the highly intellectualized myth-system required in the Platonic city. While the myth-content would be different if we were to consider cities having different habits, the process of myth formation itself would not be likely to proceed on significantly different lines. It is to be understood that the functional analysis of myth, or operative projections, gives a result which in no sense exhausts the meaning of historical myth and parable generally considered.

The conflict between individual and social interest seems inseparable from the fact that individual life is short and that social life is long. It is natural for man to adopt in his own thought and action a time-scale that is shorter than that required for continuous social life. Matters which are socially desirable, or even necessary, may involve individual sacrifice, sometimes life itself. As Plato had done his best to atomize the family, which to the common run of men is the natural bridge between the individual and society, this conflict was to him of special urgency. Society cannot adopt the short time-scale of individuals and survive; the individual, therefore, must in some way be brought to adopt the long (eternal) time-scale of society. Plato, as other founders of state, finds it expedient, therefore, to teach men that they consist of body and soul; he teaches them further that the soul is immortal: by a part of his being man is projected up to the time-scale needed for social survival. But the immortality of the soul is not, taken by itself, sufficient for the present purpose: myth (whether or not it is metaphysically or in any other sense "true") must be worked out so as to affect the temporal behavior of the subjects in the right way; Plato has to create a connection between the temporal state and the eternal state. He therefore adds to his construction an abode for departed spirits; he teaches men that their fate after death is determined by their actions in the city; the departed soul lives in a society which represents a kind of inverted outer kingdom; the life of its citizens is, as it were, in the nature of reward or punishment for earthly virtues or vices. Accepting these myths as fact it becomes quite rational for a pious man to follow social habit voluntarily and even joyfully. Behavior, that to a natural man would be folly, appears to the pious as ultimate rationality. The pious individual is thus saved from frustration and his life falls to his inner eye into a great meaningful pattern. The ruler creates good subjects and saves himself and the city from the monsters.

The power of rendering projections operative—that is, making them credible as fact—is far from absolute. Indeed, the residue of force in government is there to testify to the limitations of such powers. But even in this first statement, we have to remind ourselves again and again that social sacrifice is present and real; that future punishment is distant, if not hypothetical; that men may value present gain more than they fear distant punishment; and that while it may not be possible to eliminate these weaknesses in the construction, all must be done to minimize them. The basic projections must be raised, therefore, into the highest possible emotional potency; they must be rendered as immediate and tangible as possible. The place of departed spirits is a boldly functional construction, but Heaven and Hell have in time become so rich in feeling, and so overgrown by imagery as to surpass earthly cities in beauty both sweet and terrible. Men have become incapable of entering into the inner kingdom without awe and, as it were, a distant trembling of the soul. It evokes tenderness and longing; in it is the strange feeling of home-coming to a true being.

But, forgetting the ancient spells, we should try to understand in detail the relation between the inner kingdom and the outer. The ties that bind them together constitute, or reflect, moral ties in society. To render the inner kingdom operative the first virtue needed in the subject is belief in the social projections; for their potency decreases in direct proportion as they are doubted. Belief itself, or piety, becomes in Plato's state, as in other vertical and autocratic cities, the supreme duty to which all others must be subordinated. And according to the tale of Er, among the vices for which punishment in after life is "unusually great," first place is given to impiety; correspondingly, reward for piety is equally great. And as the ruler may be said to incarnate the outer balance of society, it is necessary next that the subjects should obey him unquestioningly and willingly. In a sense, it was to promote such obedience that the inner kingdom was originally constructed. Disobedience, therefore, is placed second among the crimes for which punishment in after life is "unusually great."

But such projections can be elaborated in almost infinite detail; let us instead of multiplying examples, listen for a moment to the great mythmaker himself: "Very well, I will speak. And yet I hardly know how to find the audacity or the words to speak and undertake to persuade first the rulers themselves and the soldiers and then the rest of the city, that in good sooth all our training and educating of them were things that they imagined and that happened to them as it were in a dream; but that in reality at that time they were down within the earth being molded and fostered themselves while their weapons and the rest of their equipment were being fashioned. And when they were quite finished the earth as being their mother delivered them, and now as if their land were their mother and their nurse they ought to take thought of her and defend her against any attack and regard the other citizens as their brothers and children of the selfsame earth.

"It is not for nothing," [said Glaucon], "that you were so bashful about coming out with your lie." [5]

The citizens are thus brethren and they are naturally bound to defend their country against external enemies. While the in-

[5] *Republic*, 414d-e.

junction to obedience was principally directed towards the function of order, this new projection is more specifically addressed to the function of defense. This feeling of brotherhood, though it is all to the good as long as it has an external object in view, would become fatal to order (which is on the vertical model) if the feeling of equality were not supplemented by a further projection justifying the internal inequalities. So Plato continues: ". . . Hear the rest of the story. While all of you in the city are brothers, we will say in our tale, yet God in fashioning those of you who are fitted to hold rule mingled gold in their generation, for which reason they are the most precious—but in the helpers silver, and iron and brass in the farmers and other craftsmen. And as you are all akin, though for the most part you will breed after your kinds, it may sometimes happen that a golden father would beget a silver son and that a golden offspring would come from a silver sire and that the rest would in like manner be born of one another. So that the first and chief injunction that the god lays upon the rulers is that of nothing else are they to be such careful guardians and so intently observant as of the intermixture of these metals in the souls of their offspring . . . [and are to] assign to each the status due to his nature . . . alleging that there is an oracle that the state shall then be overthrown when the man of iron or brass is its guardian." [6]

Having thus justified social inequality, Plato describes in a deeper vein the inner kingdom in words multiplied by echoes: "It is not, let me tell you, . . . the tale to Alcinous told that I shall unfold, but the tale of a warrior bold, Er, the son of Armenius. . . . He once upon a time was slain in battle, and . . . on the twelfth day . . . he returned to life and told what he had

[6] *Ibid.,* 415a-c.

seen in the world beyond. . . . There judges were sitting and after every judgment they bade the righteous journey to the right
and upwards through the heaven . . . and the unjust to take
the road to the left and downward . . . to tell it all, Glaucon,
would take all our time, but the sum was this. For all the wrongs
they had ever done to anyone they paid the penalty in turn ten-
fold for each. . . . If we are guided by me we shall believe
that the soul is immortal and capable of enduring all extremes
of good and evil, and so we shall hold ever to the upward way
and pursue righteousness with wisdom always and ever, that we
may be dear to ourselves and to the gods both during our sojourn
here and when we receive our reward, as the victors in the games
go about to gather in theirs. And thus both here and in that
journey of a thousand years, whereof I have told you, we shall
fare well." [7]

The tales have been retold many times; the projections,
Proteus-like, have been adapted to many cities and have been
elaborated by new fancy. Still, they remain the children of their
dark mother, necessity; they follow the rulers—shadows cast by
the too bright light of reason. And unfortunately, as the master
or a wise disciple has told us, an understanding of their nature
is not "good for people with the exception of a few who are
capable of discovering it for themselves with a minimum of
demonstration. As for the rest, I fancy that some would be
filled perversely with a misguided contempt and others with a
soaring, windy expectation—in the belief that they had learnt
something tremendous." [8]

[7] *Ibid.* 614b-621d.   [8] Plato's *Letters*, No. 7, 341e.

3

The Government

OF THE CITY

WE MUST SPEAK FIRST OF THE
MANAGEMENT OF THE HOUSEHOLD;
FOR EVERY CITY IS COMPOSED
OF HOUSEHOLDS.—*Aristotle* [1]

PLATO DISCOVERED THE SOCIAL FUNCTIONS and considered the problem of social balance under the general heading of justice. He raised the lasting questions as to the nature of social order and social structure; and in the end he became engrossed in the underlying patterns of education and myth-formation. His preoccupation with these broad issues was possible because he had entrusted the details of perceiving and imposing social balance to a perfect ruler. But as real cities have been governed by men falling far short of perfection and still managed to survive for long periods, it follows that some other arrangement must be thought of as performing the functions which Plato assigned to the perfect ruler. It is to a study of these arrangements that we now have to turn. Their importance, both practical and theoretical, is such as to require a rather careful analysis.

In his attempt to isolate the underlying social necessities, Plato constructed a city that was, it seemed, not only changeless but also

[1] *Politics,* 1253b.

as nearly atomistic as he could make it. The basic social unit was
the individual, and what intervened between the ruler and the
subject came to appear as a stumbling block on the road to perfection. But in driving his theoretical construction to this ultimate
point of vertical integration, he had also, in many respects,
estranged it from simple realities. And, says Plato's pupil, having
asked the same questions as the master: "He who . . . considers
things in their first growth and origin, whether a state or anything
else, will obtain the clearest view of them. In the first place there
must be union of those who cannot exist without each other;
namely, of male and female, that the race may continue . . . and
of natural ruler and subject, that both may be preserved. . . . Out
of these relationships between man and woman, master and slave,
the first thing to arise is the family . . . When several families
are united . . . the first society to be formed is the village. . . .
When several villages are united in a single complete community
. . . the state comes into existence, originating in the bare needs
of life, and continuing in existence for the sake of a good life." [2]
Aristotle may be right in the belief that the family originated before the city; at any rate, it can be observed that the family, rather
than the individual, has been, and continues to be, the instrumentality through which society arranges the functions of production
and reproduction. These functions are, so to speak, performed
indirectly by a system of family habit enclosed in a larger social
pattern of custom. How society is to meet these functions depends
upon the collective behavior of families rather than upon individual
actions directly controlled by rulers. The pattern of family behavior
is interposed between individual and society, and most people still
maintain their most vital social contacts through the family. In

[2] *Ibid*, 1252a-b.

order to understand how social balance is actually achieved, it is necessary, therefore, to consider, even though briefly, some characteristic traits of the behavior of families.

Though man be a social being, he must be thought of as belonging to a biological species. Nature is lavish with seed and potentialities of growth; man, like other species, was endowed with a birth rate so high that, left to itself, it leads to growth in geometric progression. Hence, if pressure of reproduction were not met by counter pressures of various kinds, population would soon increase beyond all bounds. And nature does indeed oppose an array of such counter pressures: lack of food, sickness, enemies, and so on. It establishes a rough, fluctuating, but real balance by means of a complex system of checks and counterchecks. And when the city came into being, it may be assumed that men yielded to the "instinct" of reproduction with the same disregard of consequence as other members of the animal kingdom.

Actual observation of human behavior is concerned with long-established societies. It is difficult to form reliable notions as to reproductive behavior in general, and it is particularly dangerous to interpret past behavior in the light of present behavior. Societies now called "primitive" do not necessarily represent conditions original to man; such societies have come down from antiquity, and behavior in them cannot help having been modified by long social exposure. And the more "advanced" a city is said to be, the less is behavior directly dictated by the voice of nature. But with all such reservations, experience suggests some broad conclusions.

The actual birth rates in human society have been and generally continue to be high enough to provide—if not variously checked—for increase in a geometric ratio. It is true that in some civilizations we are able to observe a conscious limitation of births; but historically speaking these are exceptional cases. Where such a break with the ways of nature has come to prevail, it leads to far-reaching social consequences, which will be considered in due course. Meanwhile, we would seem to be well within the bounds of relevant experience in assuming an *average* birth rate which (outer conditions permitting) would lead to some, however small, population increase.

It is not necessary to demonstrate that within a limited territory— and given any particular set of habits—population cannot indefinitely increase at any rate. This conclusion goes back to relationships summarized in the so-called law of diminishing returns: after a point, application of more labor and capital to a plot of land yields a decreasing proportionate return. Hence, when under equal conditions population expands in a given territory, the quantity of food and other necessaries of life produced begin to grow smaller and smaller per capita. As a result of starvation and privation of different kinds, people begin to die off faster, until deaths match births at any given level of output and consumption. Disregarding fluctuations, upwards and downwards, caused by random changes in economic and demographic factors, equilibrium between births and deaths will be reached at the point where the level of consumption is the same as the minimum of existence in a stable population. This general relationship can also be expressed so that population numbers tend to become determined by the quantity of the means of sustenance, and so indirectly by the productive function.

Given these conditions of stable habit and territory, population would, in the long run, establish equilibrium on the basis of a short average expectation of life. Many, or most, of the children born would fail to reach maturity; if the individual family wanted to survive, it would have to match what to it would appear an objectively given death rate with an equally high birth rate. It would be trapped into a never-ending race between deaths and births; and as long as the birth rate remained on this "natural" level, the family would unwittingly maintain a stable relationship between the social functions of production and reproduction by giving a definite and lasting priority to the function of reproduction.

Given this priority accorded to reproduction, it is thus obvious why, in the long run, the number of the population will be determined by the stream of goods and services reaching the family from the process of production. Disregarding random fluctuations, society could neither increase, nor decrease, the average level of popular consumption (per capita), which in consequence of the priority given to the reproductive function would establish itself around the minimum of existence. Rulers, therefore, inside this framework of habit, are incapable of affecting permanently the living standards of subjects. But, even if incapable of affecting the relative level of popular consumption, they may still, in many ways, influence the *absolute volume* of goods and services flowing into such consumption. In actual fact, rulers have many ways of either increasing or decreasing the stream of consumption goods; the most obvious is taxation. In few fields has human ingenuity gone further: for taxes can be in kind, money, or personal service; they can be direct or indirect; they can take the forms of bribes, loans, levies, fines, customs, and confiscations; they can be obtained by debasing the coin of the realm. But the flow of resources is perhaps even more profoundly, though less obviously, affected by the institutions of property and ownership. On the whole, all these connected institutions lead to a transfer of resources and energy from one group to another, from one function to another; we summarize these transactions under the common name of social *transfer*. In this institution the rulers have then the means of either increasing or decreasing the absolute flow of the means of sustenance available to their subjects. But as, under the conditions given, they are, in the long run, unable to affect the level of consumption, changes in the volume of transfer will lead to changes in the *number* of persons that can survive. It follows, therefore, that transfer indirectly determines population numbers, and hence the resources which can be given to the function of reproduction. But before it is possible to grasp the import of this conclusion, it is necessary to consider the uses to which transfer is put: and how these uses affect the social situation as a whole.

Imagine that in an existing city all organized government were suddenly to disappear. Each family would be thrown on its own devices. It would, we may suppose, continue to breed to the limits set by economic necessities; but in the absence of order, authority, courts, and magistrates, families would become involved in factions, thefts, arson, murder, and vendetta. Life would become insecure and the risks to property almost boundless. In this state of anarchy, productivity of labor would naturally decrease; it would cease to be profitable to engage in activities requiring long planning or capital investment. With the destruction of secure markets division of labor would cease to be practicable; the flow of products would dry up and become more uneven and sporadic; for as insecurity increased, the laying up of stocks would become too hazardous and food supply would fluctuate greatly between seasons and years. Periods of relative plenty would be followed by periods of famine. In consequence, population numbers would begin to fluctuate more violently than before.

It would be in the interest of all, therefore, to reestablish order. But this requires the expenditure of social energies and resources in the formation of a special system of habit. It requires the training of men in certain skills, and these men must be provided with the tools needed for their craft. If some man, or some group of men, were asked to reintroduce order in the state, they would, *ipso facto,* have a claim on society's resources and depend upon transfer. In this light, transfer shows up as the price that society has to pay for the performance of the function of order. The efficiency of the system as a whole depends upon the integration of several necessary parts; and as order is such a part, it would be superficial to claim that transfer as such represents social waste (though, of course, it may be misused or wasted) or that it can be arbitrarily imposed or removed. In a more narrow sense, as productivity of labor is a function of the social system as a whole, transfer may even be considered as a cost of production *au pair* with other necessary costs. At any rate, it is illogical to deny order an independent claim on the social resources. In historical society the function of order is entrusted, on the whole, to special groups in possession of special rights and prerogatives among which are the powers of transfer.

But even if transfer is a necessary and constituent part of the city, the question remains how far it should be carried and, more generally, what its relation may be to the social balance. The answer to these questions is implicit in the mode of analysis which is familiar to the classical economist. If the introduction of order increases productivity, it may be assumed that the first "unit of order" yields a return greater than its cost in terms of transfer; so it is likely to go for several successive units of order; but sooner or later there comes a point where the addition to the social product is equal to its cost in transfer: this is the marginal point after which further additions to order will decrease the social product. Transfer and expansion of order should then be driven just to this optimum point, but no further: at this point transferable surplus reaches its maximum. In the theoretical model the optimum is represented by a specific point: in reality, of course, one would have to deal with a rather broad area. For not only would it be difficult to determine statistically this point with any precision but it would also change with changes in habit, with the greater or smaller ability of rulers, and with waste of different kinds.

We have thus found that the wise ruler should drive transfer exactly to the point where it maximizes long-term transferable surplus. A perfect ruler would easily perceive this, and unselfishly try to carry out such a policy in practice. But actual rulers are, perhaps, neither wise nor good; and it is not clear how they, without provoking immediate disaster, can be entrusted with the control of the levers of transfer; it would seem to be in their natural interest to maximize transfer at once and thus their own riches and power. In order to resolve such doubts, consider then the penalties attached to the misuse of transfer. Assume first that transfer is carried beyond the optimum point. The stream of goods and services available for popular consumption would then decrease absolutely, leading, in turn, to a contraction of population; for as the standard of living is already at the level of the minimum of existence, changes in popular consumption are inevitably translated into changes in population numbers. And population would go on contracting as long as transfer went beyond its optimum point. But a continuous population contraction leads to a parallel contraction of the national product: and in order to maintain a given absolute transfer, relative transfer must be constantly increased in a spiral of contraction in which the ruler, so to speak, consumes the social substance itself. If the ruler is incapable of reducing transfer, or unwilling to reduce it—and faster than the loss of national product—this process will roll on to the bitter end of complete social disintegration. In reality, of course, such processes have powerful brakes in the ruler's self-interest and in the risk of revolts among the subjects. But examples of social contraction—and even social disintegration—caused by excessive transfer abound in history; and particularly in the disarmed provinces of great empires victimized by the greed of conquerors. In the empirical art of ruling—embodied in surviving practice—it is natural, therefore, that the safeguards against excessive transfer should be unusually powerful. Indeed, the right of taxation has become, in advanced cities, the most jealously guarded privilege of all.

The opposite danger—that transfer should not be driven far enough—has rather the anemic hue of academic dispute. Experience shows that rulers seem to be more eager to impose new taxes than to relax old ones. They have never lacked good reasons for driving transfer even beyond the optimum point; and they have a mighty advocate in self-interest. But if a ruler were either mild or weak enough to neglect self-interest, he would expose himself to the risk of internal revolt; and his country would, in reality, become a tempting prey for enterprising neighbors. One may conclude, therefore, that in cities which have survived for a long time, there will be a tendency for transfer to stabilize itself not too far from the theoretical optimum point, which also coincides with the ruler's long-time (as opposed to his short-time) interest.

We have gathered together a number of old and well-known facts and relationships. But the feeling of familiarity should not dim our perception of the lesson which they try to impart when united. For before us we have nothing less than a kind of mechanism which explains how outer social balance can be maintained without the benefit of perfect rulers—and even the consciousness of social ends. In so far as families give "natural" priority to the function of reproduction, transfer will automatically determine the amount of social resources and energies that will be given to each social function (excluding, in a closed society, the function of defense). Given the system of habit, transfer determines the total national product, and the part of it that goes to each function. The most stable balance (characterized by maximum income per head) is reached when a ruler follows his own self-interest, and maximizes transfer that can be obtained, not over a short period, but over a long period of time. Transfer can be considered in the nature of a regulator of the outer social balance of the city, and thus as a determining factor in the life of the city itself. Aristotle, therefore, considered as rulers (or citizens) all those who either directly through taxation, or indirectly through the institution of property, had the power to dispose of the city's "revenue," and thus to determine the use of resources for functions other than production and reproduction. These elements are together the guardians of the social balance: and "that some should rule," he says, "and others be ruled is a thing not only necessary but expedient; from the hour of their births some are marked for subjection, others for rule." [3] It is inevitable, therefore,

[3] Aristotle, *Politics*, 1254a.

that "states consist of two classes, of poor men and rich" and founders of states, having in mind the vertical construction of society, conceive order as resting on the division of the city: the multitude of the poor moving in the never-broken circle of reproduction and toil; the rulers, the rich, toiling not and controlling the levers of transfer, ruling, if not composing, the state properly understood.

But the critical function and the central position of transfer give rise to a further question. The city of Plato (and the city of Aristotle) borrowed, we said, its system of habit from the Hellenic city-state. It was, relatively speaking, highly developed and the productivity of its labor must be conceived as relatively high. But if—as we have just observed—there exists a natural interdependence between social organization and labor productivity, it follows that the productivity of labor, taken for granted by Plato, was in fact the fruit of previous historical development. It can reasonably be expected that if we were to go further back in time, we would strike less efficient habits of production, administration, and so on. Undertaking an imaginary journey back in time, we would strike an ultimate point where labor productivity would be just high enough to keep the laborer himself supplied with the necessaries of life. If such a situation were to prevail—as on the tundra, the high mountains, or the desert— no continuous social life would be at all possible. Hence, survival of man requires a labor productivity at least high enough to permit the laborer to produce what is needed to keep his race stable. This point represents, therefore, the theoretical level beneath which life, for any biological species, is impossible. An understanding of this relationship is essential to social theory; it unmasks, to start with, a paradox inherent in all evolved social life.

For, if at this critical point the laborer works "all his time to produce the necessary means of subsistence for himself and his race, he has no time left in which to work gratis for others. Without a certain degree of productiveness in his labour, he has no . . . superfluous time at his disposal; without such superfluous time, no surplus labour, and therefore no capitalists, no slave-owners, no feudal lords, in one word, no class of large proprietors." [4] Thus transfer, and with transfer the vertical integration of society, presupposes a labor productivity which already lies above the critical point. In other words, giving the name *social surplus* to that part of the social product which is not required in order to maintain the race stable and which, accordingly, is available for transfer, it follows that Plato had taken for granted a labor productivity high enough to supply a surplus sufficient unto the many purposes of his state. But "no mystical ideas must in any way be connected, as sometimes happens, with the historically developed productiveness of labour. It is only after men have raised themselves above the rank of animals, when therefore their labour has been to some extent socialized, that a state of things arises in which the surplus-labour of the one becomes a condition of existence for the other. . . . Productiveness of labour . . . is a gift, not of nature, but of history embracing thousands of centuries." [5] We are to all appearances, caught in a dilemma which renders all social emergence miraculous. For it is impossible, we are told, to construct a city without a previous labor productivity high enough to permit a social surplus transferable to uses other than the mere maintenance of population; but such labor productivity, we are told too, is the fruit only of

[4] Karl Marx, *Capital* (The Modern Library, New York, 1906), p. 561.
[5] *Ibid.,* pp. 561–562.

previous social development. The Marxian dilemma points to the terra incognita of social origins, and must be taken seriously by any consistent social theory. But for the moment we leave this critical area of theory, and return to the model of a city already endowed with a developed habit-system.

4

The Virtue

OF THE CITY

NEITHER BY NATURE, THEN, NOR CONTRARY
TO NATURE DO VIRTUES ARISE IN US; RATHER
WE ARE ADAPTED BY NATURE TO RECEIVE
THEM, AND ARE MADE PERFECT BY HABIT. . . .
IT MAKES NO SMALL DIFFERENCE, THEN,
WHETHER WE FORM HABITS OF ONE KIND OR
OF ANOTHER FROM OUR VERY YOUTH; IT
MAKES A VERY GREAT DIFFERENCE OR
RATHER *all* THE DIFFERENCE.—*Aristotle* [1]

THE INSTITUTION OF TRANSFER came to determine the outer balance
of the city; it was implicit in the fact of government itself whether
or not its significance was realized by either rulers or ruled. Optimum transfer (securing lasting social balance) occurred when
rulers, guided by their long-term interest, maximized total transfer over the long period. But rulers may be carried away by
greed and passion and forget their long-time interest in favor
of greater immediate satisfaction. As long as we have reason to
fear such weakness in rulers, the city continues to be in danger.

In the Republic the dangerous privilege of choice was reserved
for a single ruler. But even so, Plato did not feel that he had

[1] *Nicomachean Ethics,* 1103a-b.

altogether eliminated the danger of arbitrary, and irrational, choice. A ruler, he feared, may become infected by the "silly and foolish notion of happiness." A ruler, he predicted, would be born in the course of time under a wrong constellation of stars; he would stray from the path of reason and succumb to desire; he would set in motion a fatal process ending in the decay of the city in the double embrace of anarchy and tyranny. Plato himself would then seem to bid us to find safeguards for the social balance more powerful than the direct rule of reason. In effect, to trust in a single man is a declaration of war upon the law of probability—a declaration that no practical founder of a state can wittingly afford to issue. Thus, while Aristotle was not the first to observe the weakness in the Platonic construction, he was the first to point to an alternative, or rather complementary, method by which the danger of arbitrary choice could be reduced even if not completely eliminated. Aristotle was steeped in practical affairs of state and taught by experience and was ever conscious of the power constellations in actual states: it is impossible, he thought, to achieve stable government in opposition to the most powerful elements; thus the ruling element should embrace all those who directly through taxation, or indirectly through the institution of property, are in a position to affect the social balance by means of transfer. It should include the kings (if any), the magistrates, the judges, the civil servants, the soldiers, and the priests, but also the merchants and property-holders.

The ruling element in an evolved city is far from homogeneous: it is composed of many groups which, while all are nourished from the social surplus in other respects, have different functions, interests, outlook, and training. Most, if not all revolutions are caused by factional strifes in the ruling element—in the same

manner as most constitutions arise from a different distribution
of power within it. Rulers can temporarily acquire greater wealth
and power by driving transfer beyond the optimum point; factions within the ruling element can increase their wealth and
power by acquiring a larger part of a common transfer. The
rewards of such a course of action are immediate and visible; the
punishments distant and general. Will then, asks Aristotle, a
group vested with such powers and temptations be satisfied with
mere "life"? Will not, in time, the pursuit of life be followed
by the pursuits of property and happiness, in fine, a "good life"
as conceived by common men?

Thus, while Aristotle agrees with the Master that the city
is created for survival, coming into being for the sake of life, he
adds that it can continue "in existence for the sake of a good life."
This qualification could perhaps be interpreted in the normative
sense of *summum bonum*. But the "good life" is reserved for
the ruling element, belonging not like "life" to the whole of the
city, but to a part of it only. This seems to imply that "good life"
is conceived rather as a means than as an end of social life. We
accept this more literal interpretation, retaining life as ultimate
postulate (of which logically there can be hardly more than one),
while adding "good life," as a condition for (or a means of)
continuous social "life." And in this light, it becomes easy to
understand how the philosopher can consistently use the concept
of the "good life" as the framework within which he tries to
harmonize and stabilize the behavior of the ruling elements.

In order to prevent misunderstanding it may be added that we
are aware that Aristotle is a philosopher difficult to pin down.
No particular construction is wide enough to contain the full
richness of life, and Aristotle is less than most men a prisoner of

his own intellect. It is quite possible, basing oneself on textual authority, to derive from him social theories of different natures. But pursuing our own ends within the framework of a theoretical model, it seems legitimate to isolate and develop the rationalist line of thought obviously present in Aristotelian philosophy. What follows should not then be considered as an attempt to explain the full meaning of Aristotle's political philosophy. We borrow here from his writings such authentic elements as are needed in pursuing our inquiry into the social relationships, just as we shall later depend on other elements in order to develop other lines of thought.

At first sight Aristotle's task appears even more difficult than that of Plato. If Plato could not steel a single ruler against the temptation of arbitrary choice, how can Aristotle control the behavior of a large heterogeneous element? Still, it is necessarily to the organization and training of this element that he now must turn. In order to understand the following construction it is useful to consider the new concept of virtue. Plato considered a just man one who in each situation acted according to the dictate of social reason in the interest of the whole. Justice was thus defined in terms of reasonable action, emerging in each instance from a conscious process. Virtue, according to Aristotle, may perhaps be understood as the pattern of human behavior which if collectively adopted serves the good of the whole, rather than the good of the part. But virtue is an ambiguous word and Aristotle distinguishes between intellectual and moral virtue. "Intellectual virtue in the main owes both its birth and its growth to teaching (for which reason it requires experience and time), while moral virtue comes about as the result of habit, whence also its name *ethike* is one that is formed by a slight variation from the word, *ethos* (habit). . . . Legislators make the citizens good by forming habits in them." [2] And in a later connection he adds: "There are three things which make men good and virtuous: these are nature, habit, and rational principle." [3]

It is not easy to discover any significant difference between the Platonic concept of justice and the Aristotelian concept of intellectual virtue: for, indeed, says Aristotle: "Justice belongs to the City, justice is an ordering of the political association, and justice is a selecting of what is just." [4] The determination of intellectual virtue and justice is the common work of social reason. The content of morals and virtue can be determined, not by reference to habit or nature, but only with reference to "rational principle" in society. Hence, it is apparent that the difference between master and pupil, if any, relates not to how justice (or intellectual virtue) should be determined but only to how they should be made socially operative.

Plato entrusted the social balance, and thus the determination of justice in each case, to the administration of a perfect ruler. He required, therefore, in his philosopher king nothing less than a "revolution in the soul" which freed him from the old tyrannies of passion and custom. Aristotle entrusted this office, not to administrators of the city, but to some legislator or founder of state. For by creating a wise constitution and training the citizens in certain ways he could create virtue in them by habituation rather than by intense cultivation of reason. Aristotle discovered between the peaks of rational principle and the valleys of natural behavior a middle ground where men live virtuously because of the character stamped upon them by wise training. Hence, should a legislator, just as the perfect ruler, be able, guided by rational

[2] *Nicomachean Ethics,* 1103a-b,   [3] *Politics,* 1132a.   [4] *Ibid.,* 1253a.

principle, to determine the right content of virtue—that is, of social habit—he could by training the citizens in certain ways create in them a character which would make it natural for them to live virtuously. We encounter the social institution of character-formation, and let us continue in the philosopher's own words: "Again, of all things that come to us by nature we first acquire the potentiality and later exhibit the activity . . . ; but virtues we get by first exercising them, as also happens in the case of the arts as well. For the things we have to learn before we can do them, we learn by doing them, e.g., men become builders by building and lyre-players by playing the lyre; so too we become just by doing just acts, temperate by doing temperate acts, brave by doing brave acts. . . . Thus, in one word, states of character arise out of like activities." [5] It is thus by training—by reflexes stabilized and conditioned by stimuli of pleasure and pain—that the legislator instills virtuous behavior that is both individually and socially acceptable. The obedience to social necessity becomes a habit, withdrawn from the need of conscious determination. Virtue, instead of opposing habit, profits from the collective might of habit. With Aristotle, habituation becomes an essential part of social theory.

Returning to the relation of the concept of the "good life" to the city, it is the task of the legislator to determine the right system of habit, and thus the forms of individual behavior fitted to them. And as the concept of "good life" is aimed at the creation of right character in the ruling element, it is necessary to understand on one hand the functions of this element, and on the other hand the deep gulf that separates it from the multitude. There is no significant difference between Plato and Aristotle in their

[5] *Nicomachean Ethics*, 1103a-b.

way of conceiving the nature and functions of the multitude. It remains a mere instrument of state; and by supplying the means of a "good life" to the rulers it contributes to the survival of the whole.

The purpose of the legislator is to create in the ruling element a character that prevents arbitrary and appetitive life in the rulers. But whatever the content of "good life" may turn out to be, Aristotle found rightly that training in virtue was a long process which required, among other things, a certain liberty from manual toil. The habituation in virtue, or the education in citizenship, required, therefore, resources which could be drawn only from the social surplus through the means of transfer. In any given social system, surplus—and thus possible transfer—is numerically determinate. The quantity of goods and services which can be used for the purposes of "good life" is thereby given; and the size of the ruling elements becomes inversely proportionate to its level of living. The higher the latter the smaller their numbers and vice versa. In the *Republic* the distribution of surplus was achieved under the guidance of a perfect ruler, and Plato had little occasion to consider this problem. To Aristotle it is of crucial importance.

In the atomistic and rationalistic construction of the *Republic,* communism was the reply to the problem of distribution. But with the delegation of the social functions of production and reproduction to the family, this solution breaks down and becomes, at any rate, impossible of administration. The family— in virtue of its delegated function of production—must also dispose of the means of production. The question of property and its distribution (given the system as a whole) determines in the last analysis the social surplus, in such a way that both the size and the level of living of the ruling element largely become a function of the distribution of property. The wider the distribution of property the larger and poorer becomes the ruling element and vice versa. In theory, the right distribution seems easy to determine—as easy, in fact, as it is difficult in practice. The stability of the state requires a ruling element numerically large enough to oppose revolutions and the power of factions. Aristotle favors a strong middle element in the state by fixing property qualifications, and hence the level of living of the ruling element, at the minimum which is required for a life of "activity according to virtue." He has thereby laid down the limits for a "good life."

In practice, therefore, the determination of the social structure depends upon how much wealth and leisure is required for training in virtue. Opinions on this matter will necessarily differ and are affected by the more or less advanced, the more or less complex, state of habit; but more important than theoretical precision in this respect is that property qualifications, once fixed, should not be changed. "Men should guard against the beginning of transgression," [6] and stability would be threatened by "a plunge into an unbounded acquisition of wealth" as much as by a pauperization of the ruling elements. A certain level of living—including such luxury and display as may be seemly or necessary—must be taken for granted; and any change in such levels should be considered unseemly and impious. But such stability imposes some special requirements on the rulers. We found that the multitude should breed up to the natural limit, and social stability requires that they continue to do so; indeed, it is implicit in a standard of living at the level of the minimum of existence. But if the "good life"

[6] *Politics,* 1307b.

requires a level of living above this minimum, it is necessary to restrict its natural tendency of increase. "One would have thought," says Aristotle, "that it was even more necessary to limit population, and to prevent reproduction from exceeding a certain level, than to limit property. If population is limited, the rate of reproduction should be fixed to allow for the incidence of infant mortality and for the amount of infertility among married couples. If no restriction is imposed on the rate of reproduction (and this is the case in most of our existing states), poverty is the inevitable result; and poverty produces, in its turn, revolution and crime." [7] Hence, "the legislator who fixes the amount of property should also fix the number of children." [8] And, continues the Philosopher: "In our state population has a limit . . . no child is to be exposed, but when couples have children in excess, let abortion be procured before sense and life have begun." [9] Late marriages would tend to the same result; and adding certain other factors (war, primogeniture, migration, etc.) it is possible, though perhaps not likely, that the legislator will achieve a certain numerical stability in the ruling element.

Having thus circumscribed the content and function of the "good life" it is time to consider how the ruling elements shall be habituated to meet its function and acquire a social character. We can do no better than again listen to Aristotle: "The many, of whom each individual is but an ordinary person, when they meet together may very likely be better than the few good, if regarded not individually but collectively, just as a feast to which many contribute is better than a dinner provided out of a single purse . . . the many . . . may become in a manner one man, who has many feet, and hands, and senses, also many qualities

[7] *Ibid.,* 1265b.   [8] *Ibid.,* 1166b.   [9] *Ibid.,* 1335b.

of character and intelligence. . . . Whether this principle can apply . . . to all bodies of men is not clear. Or rather, by heaven, in some cases it is impossible of application. . . . But there may be bodies of men about whom our statement is nevertheless true." [10]

Virtue, it seems then, does not pertain to a random assembly of people. A mob of brutes cannot be expected to exercise virtuous action; far more than a single ruler, it would be swayed by winds of passion and madness. To become capable of deliberation and action according to virtue, a group must through habituation be made into a true union of citizens having norms of behavior, a sense of obligation and a character in common. Such character is more than manners uncomfortably put on, as when a man of base birth comes to visit in a noble house; the role to which the citizen is called must be felt by him as an expression of his own nature. He should conceive the answers to the perennial questions as eternal verities. Virtue, being habit, is most secure when it needs no defense; well-bred manners, a strict code of honor, and desire for seemly action are here preferable to cleverness. A true union of citizens tends to the mean and instinctively expels the truly good or the truly bad. On matters of public concern it speaks with the authentic voice of the gods of the city.

A union of citizens represents a new kind of social order. In the Platonic city we likened order to that imposed by a gardener on nature. Social events were the result of orders issued by a ruler. But in this new state we find social events arranging themselves, as it were, spontaneously in socially determined patterns: order is contained in the character of the citizens who are joined by training in common habit. We designate this kind of order as

[10] *Ibid.,* 1281b.

natural order: it has many a correspondence in nature; a forest rests in its own ecological balance; if disturbed it reverts in time to its virginal state; iron particles in a magnetic field arrange themselves in patterns. To illustrate this principle in society let us consider a town lacking all regulations pertaining to traffic. If traffic reached a certain intensity there would develop constant traffic snarls and police would be required to keep it moving. Order would have to be imposed. But if some legislator trained people to keep to the right, and give precedence to traffic from the right, this habit would form traffic into predictable, easy-moving streams. Such forms of natural order, or virtue, are not the invention of theorists. Indeed, it is doubtful whether or not any society could exist depending altogether on rational principle and direct rule.

Granting the legislator the insight and power to form right habit, we see no particular reason why he should not succeed in joining the rulers into a true union of citizens. He would create a stable virtuous character in the citizens, and a habit of submissive toil in the multitude. Both constructions would be kept together by myth supporting habit. And as habit would be meaningful in terms of ruling myth there is no reason why the city should not rest safe in a lasting inner and outer balance. When habit and myth agree to guard a given social balance they seem invincible. In the formal sense—granting that is the condition upon which this model rests—it appears that the city has met the conditions of survival.

But the reservation is important. The conclusion represents in fact little more than a first statement of the conditions of survival. It does not appraise the probabilities as to whether or not they will or can be met in reality. There may be dangers to the city of which we are yet unaware. But before looking around for such outside dangers, we have to consider a weakness inherent in the model itself.

In creating his union of citizens, virtuously guarding the social balance through wise and moderate use of the institution of transfer, Aristotle would perhaps seem to have removed the danger to the state represented by the arbitrary action of a single ruler. But the perfect ruler—or personification of Social Reason—had not been really made away with. He had only, so to speak, been moved backstage, to become, in the person of the legislator, the invisible director of the play. The legislator has to lay down the rules of the game. And why should it be more easy to find a perfect legislator than a perfect ruler? And the punishment for finding neither a perfect ruler nor a perfect legislator is the same: nonsurvival. And to the extent that the likelihood of finding truly rational rulers and legislators is viewed pessimistically, to this extent do we, in the present model, view with misgiving the actual probabilities of social survival.

In aiming at a first statement of the social-survival problem, we assumed an "initial state" of habit. We had to bring simultaneously on the stage many historical forces draped in broad concepts. They played their appointed parts on the stage and governed the city. No philosopher conceived these concepts as more than representatives of laws and tendencies, or more briefly necessities, inherent in order. These necessities stretch their roots far back in time. And working our way towards a more realistic statement of the problem, we have to put the social mechanisms in that flux of circumstance that is life. The order of events is important. And the very concepts of Social Reason and social ends are not, as far as we have any possibility of knowing, innate to man. Social balances, we must believe, were contained in habit and guarded by myth, long before they could have become subjects of speculation and systematic theory. The first model city represents, as it were, on a single plane, shadows of events which occur in a many-dimensional reality. But it is one thing to study a mechanism already in operation; quite another to grasp the processes involved in its invention and manufacture. It is time to leave the guidance of perfect rulers and legislators, and study what happens when we leave the protective walls of the "initial state" of the model.

Our next task is to visualize the city *in statu nascendi;* and to follow it on its journey through time from the beginning to the end. And if we have found that "before virtue the gods have set sweat," [11] we shall find that before birth they have set pain. But we shall find, too, that upon the birth of the city out of nature they have let descend a merciful amnesia erasing all memory.

[11] Hesiod, *Works and Days,* line 289.

5

Division

OF THE CITY

PRIMITIVE ACCUMULATION
PLAYS IN POLITICAL ECONOMY
ABOUT THE SAME PART AS
ORIGINAL SIN IN THEOLOGY.—*Karl Marx* [1]

AFTER THE PHILOSOPHER HAD SURVEYED cities and constitutions he tried to build a perfect city of his own, and began by bringing together elements "which every state may be said to need": "First, . . . food; secondly, arts . . . ; thirdly, . . . arms; fourthly, . . . a certain amount of revenue; fifthly, or rather first . . . a care of religion; sixthly, . . . a power of deciding what is in the public interest"; [2] and seventhly, we add, children. Translating these terms, and arranging them systematically, we arrive at the following scheme:

1. The Outer Kingdom (habits)
   (*a*) Balance between habits representing the functions of production, reproduction, defense, and order (based on "arts").
   (*b*) Institution of transfer (revenue).
   (*c*) Social surplus (implied above in *b*).

---

[1] *Capital* (The Modern Library, New York, 1906), p. 784.
[2] Aristotle, *Politics,* 1328b.

  2. The Inner Kingdom (beliefs)

    (*d*) Systems of projections (religion.)

While the social institutions have grown since Plato founded the Republic, the outer balance retains the original primacy. Plato required, for his purpose, a highly centralized, atomistic state; but he lacked the administrative skills required for actually ruling it. Aristotle's reforms of the city were aimed at remedying this weakness and concerned chiefly the problems of practical government. He, being of a more practical turn of mind, recognized the basic importance of the family and delegated the functions of production and reproduction to it, and let transfer of resources take place from the mass of families to a class of citizens, or rulers. With a given set of social habits, stable balance occurs at the point of maximum income per head, a point at which transfer was also at a long-time maximum. These magnitudes were absolute, not relative. Transfer became the regulator of the outer balance because it gave determinate value to all the social functions. Misuse of this power became perhaps the greatest single danger to the state, and measures had to be taken to stabilize transfer as closely as possible to the theoretical optimum. As control over transfer belonged to the ruling element alone, the legislator had to provide different arrangements for the productive multitude and for the citizens.

The multitudes inherited the traditions from the Republic, for they remained mere means and could not escape this fate as long as they, with the natural family, gave priority to the function of reproduction. This behavior guaranteed that the level of consumption would approximate, in the long run, the minimum of existence; and rulers could neither increase nor decrease the per capita consumption of the multitude. But by increasing or decreasing total transfer, they determined the absolute stream of goods and services available for popular consumption and thus the absolute size of population. In order to render the mass of men amenable to the necessities of rule, the ruler had to project myths which justified, in individual terms, the subordination of individual interest to general interest. In the absence of such projections, frustration breeds monsters which at a point destroy the social balance either directly in anarchy, or indirectly in a preventive overexpansion of the physical arm of order. Hence, the reformed city continues Platonic in essence; it remains vertical in structure, hierarchic and, in the vulgar parlance, totalitarian.

The ruling element, or the citizens, were not altogether withdrawn from the rule of necessity, but they were exposed to the privilege and danger of arbitrary choice in some matters—a fact to be provided for in the constitution. The legislator had on the one hand to prevent a too large total transfer to the body of citizens and on the other hand a factional strife within it. Citizens, in other words, must be induced to exercise "abstinence" in the use of the resources actually or potentially at their command. The Philosopher had little or no confidence in the restraint and rationality of a single ruler, and looked for more stability in a union of citizens. The social balance was most secure, he thought, when rule was entrusted to the whole of the ruling element and when this element itself was as large as was consistent with a level of consumption necessary for training in virtue. A union of citizens would arise when each citizen had been trained in common virtue, molded in common forms of character, and habituated in common activity useful to the whole. And because such training required freedom from toil, the size of the ruling element became a func-

tion of the level of living and the quantity of surplus available
for transfer. But failing complete realization of this theoretical
optimum, it was even more important that the level of living, once
fixed, should not be changed; it is essential that the citizens should
cease to strive for more honor and wealth, and that they should
remain stable in numbers; population stability on the upper level
should be safeguarded by limitations of births, by outflux of surplus citizens, or by both these means.

If rational principle, which is also the author of justice, is free
to determine the content of virtue, there seems to be no reason
why habit and myth should not fall into harmony, and no reason,
barring outside change, why the city should not be safe in a stable
outer and inner balance. Granting these assumptions, we have
in the formal sense laid down the laws of a surviving city. But
the nature of the assumptions at once indicates the limitations of
the construct. Plato did not succeed in securing a succession of rational rulers for the Republic. Aristotle asked the legislator, or the
founder of the state, to take the place of the perfect ruler; but
he was no more able than Plato to show how perfect dignitaries
of this sort could be procured. Hence, the difference in behavior
between actual and perfect rulers and legislators becomes the
measure of the risk of social disintegration in actual states. Master and pupil discerned the elements of states with such insight
that little has been added; most revolutions and reforms have
involved little more than a reshuffling of these elements as in a
game of cards. Plato and Aristotle let rational principle—variously
disguised—begin the deal, and on their authority we have let this
fiction pass. Their cities were already conscious of "social ends"
and thus of good and evil. This theoretical procedure was justified
by the nature of the inquiry. It is wise to start with what is fa-

miliar to experience rather than with what in the nature of things cannot be observed. And the initial use of such fictions may not be very harmful. Enduring cities must in one way or the other have met objective necessities, only later discerned by reason. Their structure cannot be altogether arbitrary. Hence the emerging cities may, like living organisms in general, be analyzed as if they were subject to reason. Such an analysis is useful as a first approach if we leave a sufficiently wide margin for what is accidental and even irrational.

But in a comprehensive view of society social ends cannot be conceived as an original endowment of man. The consciousness of such ends, we must believe, emerges out of the social process itself, and we cannot longer assume therefore that the city from the outset was guided by social theory. It therefore becomes necessary to penetrate beyond the façade of habit and myth.

The great observers of society have told us that man is a social animal: habit forms human character and becomes as it were "second nature"; and sequences of habits are formed into systems representing society in its outer aspect. At this juncture, therefore, it becomes necessary to consider the nature of habit. Penetrating into the obscure regions of first origins, we shall lean heavily on the guidance of the latest great master of our tradition, Henri Bergson. Inevitably from the moment of birth we slip into a system of habits which is already waiting for us. We are expected to make it unquestioningly our own, for no family can afford to leave a child without some care and some, even if rudimentary, education. "We are hardly conscious of this; there is no effort. A road has been marked out by society; it lies open before us, and we follow it: it would take more initiative to cut across country." [3]

[3] Bergson, *The Two Sources of Morality and Religion,* p. 11.

The child is in subtle, and less subtle, ways conditioned to respond
to social stimuli and thus to acquire a social nature. The power
of habit is manifest to observation; but we know also from a common inner experience that this power of habit is, in the subject,
felt as obligation, and "we have any number of particular obligations, each calling for a separate explanation. It is natural, or
more strictly speaking, a matter of habit to obey them all." [4] And
we can, therefore, "conceive obligation as weighing on the will
like a habit, each obligation dragging behind it the accumulated
mass of the others, and utilizing thus for the pressure it is exerting
the weight of the whole: here you have the totality of obligation
for a simple, elementary, moral conscience. That is the essential:
that is what obligation could, if necessary, be reduced to, even in
those cases where it attains its highest complexity." [5] And it is
important to note that obligation is the subjective response to
habit; while it would seem natural to assign habit to the operation of obligation, this would involve us in circular reasoning.
"We go back to obligation by rational ways [but] it does not
follow that obligation was of a rational order. . . . And, after
all, however much we may reason in each particular case, formulate the maxim, enunciate the principle, deduce the consequences:
if desire and passion join in the discussion, if temptation is strong,
if we are on the point of falling, if suddenly we recover ourselves,
what was it that pulled us up? A force asserts itself which we
have called the 'totality of obligation': the concentrated extract,
the quintessence of innumerable specific habits of obedience to
the countless particular requirements of social life. This force is
no one particular thing and, if it could speak (whereas it prefers
to act), it would say: 'you must because you must.' . . . Because

[4] *Ibid.,* p. 13.   [5] *Ibid.,* pp. 16–17.

in a reasonable being reason does indeed intervene as a regulator to assure this consistency between obligatory rules or maxims, philosophy has been led to look upon it as a principle of obligation. We might as well believe that the fly-wheel drives the machinery." [6] Hence, corresponding to a system of surviving habit there comes to correspond a totality of obligation which in its pure form expresses itself as an absolute categorical imperative— "you must because you must." It matters little how we classify the sequences of social events—folkways, customs, mores, habits, etc.—they are all included in this generality of obligation. And even in a society spontaneously emerged, the system of habit has to pass the test of survival and meet the necessities of that society. There is nothing to prevent us from considering habit and its echo, obligation, as if they were rational forces expressing social necessity. And the biologist would now be on the road which would lead deeper into the instinct behavior of some animal societies.

But man, for better or worse, is also a rational animal. When he is called by the voice of obligation, he has a subjective choice of coming or not coming. And "an intelligent being generally exerts his influence on himself through the medium of intelligence." [7] And while "the more, in human society, we delve down . . . to reach obligation in general, the more obligation will tend to become necessity, the nearer it will draw, to its peremptory aspect, to instinct. And yet we should make a great mistake if we tried to ascribe any particular obligation, whatever it might be, to instinct. What we must perpetually recall is that no one obligation being instinctive, obligation as a whole *would have been* instinct if human societies were not, so to speak, bal-

[6] *Ibid.*, pp. 14–15.   [7] *Ibid.*, p. 14.

lasted with mobility and intelligence." [8] And whatever the ultimate answer may be to the question of the freedom of the human will, man responds to obligation as if faced with choice and, hence, liberty. There is an ancient feud between reason and obligation, and in order to understand how society in the midst of it can arrive at some *modus vivendi,* we must consider the nature of intelligence. We declared it to be in the nature of means-end relationships and a faculty of choice. "What then will intelligence do? It is a faculty used naturally by the individual to meet the difficulties of life; it will not follow the direction of a force which, on the contrary, is working for the species, and if it considers the individual at all, does so in the interest of the species. It will make straight for selfish decisions. But this will be only its first impulse. It cannot avoid reckoning with the force of which it feels the invisible pressure. . . . It will build up a theory of ethics in which the interpenetration of personal and general interests will be demonstrated, and where obligation will be brought back to necessity." [9] We are thrown back into the famous conflict between general and private interest; the former represented by obligation, the latter by the freedom of the intellect. Whatever the virtues of the intellect, it makes its entry on the social stage as a force hostile to the interest of the whole; it is only in the leading-strings of experience that it converts itself—in the persons of philosophers and founders of state—into social reason. But the divorce between intelligence and self is a slow, painful, and never completely successful achievement of an elite.

The best that can be done in the circumstances is to call for a mediator between obligation and intellect. Social reason, or call it the necessity of survival, had to intervene. "So that if intelligence

[8] *Ibid.,* p. 20.   [9] *Ibid.,* p. 83.

was to be kept at the outset from sliding down a slope which was dangerous to the individual and society, it could be only by the statement of apparent facts, by the ghosts of facts; failing real experience, a counterfeit experience had to be conjured up. A fiction, if its image is vital and insistent, may indeed masquerade as perception and in that way prevent or modify action. A systematically false experience, may indeed stop it pushing too far the conclusion it deduces from a true experience." [10] So *"looked at from this first point of view, religion is then a defensive reaction of nature against the dissolvent power of intelligence."* [11] We are returned in more general terms to the necessity of myth. But, as seen before, reason becomes also the dissolvent of myth when it discovers the discrepancy between myth and fact. To each myth corresponds a special belief; and to all myths a totality of belief which supports and strengthens the belief in all myths. And in any time-tested system of habit the myth-making faculty has supplied the projections required to rationalize, in individual terms, socially tolerable behavior. And as the failure, of any society, to have created the necessary projections would lead to nonsurvival, we have no other choice than to assume that in the beginning there was a fusion of habit and myth, obligation and belief. Necessity would stamp with identical images man and society.

With the dawn of self-conscious reason man begins to weave the double web of obligation and belief to protect any habit system capable of survival once it has come into being. It seems reasonable to assume, with Marx, that men originally lacked both the skill and incentive to produce more than what is necessary in order to keep the race stable. It seems logical to infer, therefore, that it is

[10] *Ibid.,* p. 99.   [11] *Ibid.,* p. 112.

on this level of efficiency that a habit system first becomes protected by the social mechanisms of conservation. On this level there can be no regular surplus, hence no transfer: property in a later sense would be unknown, and so would states and churches, rulers and armies, and all that goes with a vertical integration of society. The social structure, based on the family, would be horizontal in character. And as in time the systems of habit and belief must become congruent, myth would finally be indistinguishable from "reality." Man would be free from the burden of conscious choice; he would be free from frustration; without knowledge of "progress" he would live in a kind of moral innocence, knowing neither of the twin-companions of free choice—good and evil. This construct corresponds then in all essentials to the ancient myth, divested of its dear imagery, of a golden age in the morning of time. And the same necessity that led to the construction of this myth led Marx—as so many other founders of states—to conjure up the image of the happy state of pre-society.

Arrived at this great intersection between theory and myth we should proceed with a slow carefulness. Consider first what we must not conclude. We are not interested in the historical value of a picture arrived at by means of logical construction. As theory it neither proves nor disproves such historical hypotheses as we may entertain. Still less can the picture be explained by reference to ancestral memories. The consensus between theorist and mythmaker is due rather to the similarity of their notions of human nature. The projections of the elementary notions of a pragmatic psychology will in fact always show on the screen of the past the image of a simple, unmovable society. Be this as it may, the new construct has a wider theoretical significance. The cities of Plato and Aristotle represented, in the last analysis, unstable equilibria: if seriously disturbed, they would dissolve into their elements. Now, it is hardly satisfactory to let theory end in concepts of a series of unstable, disconnected equilibria; there is need also for the concept of a stable, underlying equilibrium forming, as it were, the field of social departure and return. And the new construct, it is easy to perceive, represents exactly such a field. It can be defined as the state which will finally materialize if habit is just efficient enough to maintain the race stable, in other words, the state where no transfer is available to meet the requirements of vertical integration. Needless to say, this equilibrium can never be perfectly realized in reality; it is nothing more than a concept useful in interpreting otherwise confused sequences of events. This *state of nature* is thus a theoretical, and not a historical, concept.

In theory, therefore, cities can arise out of nature only if the productivity of labor—a function of the efficiency of the habit system as a whole—becomes high enough to provide transferable surplus. In the light of this ancient knowledge it is quite legitimate to say that the first transfer represents the root of original sin. Without this first transfer society could not exist, nor could ideas of good and evil which are inseparable from society. In the course of time, naturally, imagination has embroidered upon the pre-historic act of social emergence. We are not ambitious enough to add another theory about the unknowable, but point out only that lasting social emergence rests on the simultaneous fulfillment of several conditions. For imagine that in a state of nature a man, or a group of men, have imposed transfer on their fellows. They would, no doubt, like to prolong this situation. Intelligence in pursuit of the Freudian trinity—"power, riches, and the love of women"—would begin to consider the means. But however reason plotted, it would be frustrated unless there should occur an increase in the productivity of labor. Without it transfer would, as we have seen, lead to population contraction and an end of the experiment. Hence, permanent rule is not a matter of mere might or cunning. It cannot perpetuate itself unless the productivity of labor is lifted to a certain level. Inventions in administration may increase the productivity of the system as a whole. The order imposed—incidental to the imposition of transfer—may within limits tend to pay for transfer. At any rate, in successful attempts at city-building, productivity must grow enough to permit the maintenance of a stable or possibly increased population. As the consumption level of the multitude fluctuates around the minimum of existence, its economic level cannot become depressed; in fact, to the extent that order can be considered as a good, the lot of the many may even improve. Still, an observer—seeing the poor support the rich—would probably imagine that transfer was the "cause" of poverty.

Social emergence and social division are inseparable concepts. The rich, the rulers, become the chief actors in the drama. The poor, the multitude, have no history; they are played upon by bold men, and like a chorus they respond as the plot unfolds. But this does not mean that the rulers can improvise their parts or become the arbitrary subjects of appetite and changing passion. In their turn they are subjects of new end-means relationships and must subordinate themselves to these or cease to be rulers. It is true that the rulers were the original revolutionaries against nature, and that they are the artisans of a new order. But they must ally themselves with social reason; they are caught in its second, ethic-forming move. Their function and interests render them the lasting enemies of original habit and original myth.

And the might of nature remains as a secret power in the city. It lies in wait in the multitude and is prepared to drag man back to nature. It seems inevitable that rulers should consider human nature with suspicion and even as inherently evil. Rulers are instrumental in creating the first monsters, and however calm the social surface may in time appear, men are not long permitted to forget the lurking danger of violent upheavals. From now on survival of race depends upon mastery over the monsters. Having imposed new habit, rulers must impose corresponding myth; they must gain time during which new obligation and new belief can spin a protective web. The revolutionary turns to conservatism; but his conversion presents him with subtle problems of ever fresh actuality.

6

THE CITY
on the Road to Growth

THINK OF THE GROWTH OF CIVILIZATIONS
IN TERMS OF THE PARABLE OF THE SOWER.
THE SEEDS WHICH THE SOWER SOWS ARE
SEPARATE SEEDS: AND EVERY GRAIN HAS
ITS OWN DIFFERENT DESTINY. . . . IT IS
ONLY A RESIDUE THAT FALLS INTO GOOD
GROUND AND BRINGS FORTH FRUIT. YET
THE SEEDS ARE ALL OF ONE KIND, AND
THEY ARE SOWN BY ONE SOWER IN THE HOPE
OF OBTAINING ONE HARVEST.—*Arnold Toynbee* [1]

CITIES HAVE BEEN REPRESENTED as unstable equilibria superimposed upon an underlying stable equilibrium of nature. Social growth—or, if you prefer, structural change—can be defined, then, as the process through which society rises out of nature and moves along the path marked by successive higher equilibria. This process is dangerous, complex, and indeed paradoxical. Its beginnings are lost in prehistoric obscurity, and logical analysis has largely to take the place of historical documentation. And throughout, the phenomena of growth are easily confused with other phenomena, such as the conditions necessary for growth, the process of ad-

[1] *A Study of History,* vol. III, p. 390.

justment to the stream of shocks always emanating from nature, and so on. For whatever the first seeds of growth may be, it can occur only when certain conditions are present; in the Parable of the Sower it is found that the nature of the ground helps to determine the outcome of the harvest. Society is placed in nature and because of the permanency of "human want" is permanently dependent upon it. This dependence, and the many phenomena to which it gives rise, may appear simple but, since a neglect of them leads to serious confusion, it may be useful to consider them here at some length.

If a land is too stony, too bleak, and too barren, it fails to support the necessaries of human life, and no social life or growth is possible. It is only at a certain level of fertility that nature permits man to feed himself and his family. The tundra and the high mountains can maintain no independent, or lasting, social life. In order to render this relationship as plain as possible consider first a marginal case. Greenland has a climate so cold and barren that it supports little vegetation directly useful to men; they must gain a livelihood by hunting and fishing. In order to keep a family in game there is need of large tracts of land; in the absence of native timber, iron, and textile fibers, fishing craft are small and of limited range; the fishing area is consequently small. Hence, owing to the nature of the land and the ways of life it imposes, population cannot expand beyond narrow limits, and it is sparsely scattered over a waste area. And even if productivity per man hour were not so low, there would be little point in catching more fish or storing more venison than could be eaten before they putrefied. It would be impossible, therefore, to create more than the rudiments of a transferable surplus. But if nature prevents the rise of surplus and transfer, it also prevents the rise of vertically integrated cities. Social organization must remain centered in the family, and questions pertaining to social class, property, government, and so on, lack the meaning they assume in islands more favored by nature.

The absence of social growth is, in such cases, altogether explained by the absence of certain conditions required for growth. The "arrestment" of societies placed in such environment offers no special problem, and it would be as unnecessary as it would be ungenerous to ascribe it to some moral or spiritual deficiency peculiar to, say, the Greenlanders. It may be added that this observation does not decrease in validity because such a community, at a later stage, may enter into communications with outside, more highly developed, societies. Trade may supply missing resources, and render resources previously without value economically important in the interconnected system as a whole. Joined into a wider system of habit, the island community may increase productivity, accumulate surplus, and, in general, behave as civilized people are supposed to behave. And as the rise of society requires the availability of certain natural resources, so does the exhaustion of these resources lead to contraction of the social structure. If an island community had achieved a certain level of productivity and integration by the use of natural resources (coal, iron, top-soil, etc.) which later became exhausted, this society would, *ceteris paribus,* have to give up such institutions and such functions as were nourished from surplus. Permanent social life, therefore, requires a permanence of resources; and the conservation of resources is a silent assumption of enduring social life.

Hence, whatever level social habit may happen to have reached and whatever particular kind of resources may happen to be in demand, natural environment continues to impose definite limits on social life. And as transfer is a condition for social growth, and as a transferable surplus was first created in the rise of agriculture, the suitability of land for agriculture naturally determined where the first cities were to grow. Ancient cities grew in the fertile and rivered valleys, and civilization remains organically tied to the green and pleasant plains of Earth. At later stages transfer, originally traceable to agriculture, has permitted the growth of more complex systems of habit; in them new resources acquire economic value and help to determine the localization of new industries and populations. But through it all nature continues to place limits beyond which social growth cannot go, however far later inventions may seem to extend these limits into an unforeseeable future.

By a wise use of natural resources—made possible by social developments as a whole—cities have occasionally grown rich. It would be a mistake to consider the natural resources, which are a necessary condition for such developments, as their "cause." It is use that gives rise to value, and cities placed in an identical natural environment may be unequal in wealth and vice versa. While it is difficult to overestimate the importance of natural resources as limiting conditions of social growth, it would nevertheless constitute a major logical error to look to them for the active principle of growth. It is quite beside the point that shocks, emanating from nature, may, as any other stimulus, serve to release later developments of habit.

To prevent misunderstanding as to the concepts of the static and the dynamic in relation to the phenomena of social growth, a few remarks are here in place. Natural environment is never unchangeable in its relation to society. There is a change of season, good years are followed by bad, vegetation and even the dividing line between land and sea change in majestic cycles. The calm stream of natural events is upset by cataclysms, earthquakes, storms, and volcanic eruptions. Now, any society must like any biological species be adaptable to such upsets. No society, therefore, is or can be static in the sense of being unable to make adjustments to environment. This would imply a *rigor mortis* unthinkable in the universe that we know. Cities must have the resiliency required to meet variations in crops and climate; they must take epidemics in their strides; they must expect adversities of many kinds. All societies have to meet the pressure of population. They have, by keeping each function bounded in value, to respond to shocks by a movement oscillating between horizontal expansion and contraction. Even in a static society, therefore, the social balance has to be considered in the nature of a dynamic equilibrium.

This process of continuous adjustment which must be thought as common to both the species and surviving cities is implicit in the equilibrating movements of the social functions: it does not constitute social growth and can still less be said to be its "cause." It rather tends to prevent growth by returning cities to the stable position of its own equilibrium. Growth, on the contrary, is represented by society's movement from one such stable position to another, from one virtual equilibrium to another. And before we consider the difficult inner mechanisms of change in habit in general, it is useful to consider first the outward, more simple, mechanisms which are involved in structural change.

In a state of nature the absence of social surplus prevents, by definition, the rise of vertically integrated, or hierarchically stratified, societies. Hence as social growth involves integration, and integration surplus and transfer, growth is, in theory, inseparable from those phenomena ultimately made possible by the rise of more efficient habit—efficient, that is, in the economic aspect. But as increased labor productivity is the result of previous change in habit as a whole, we are again returned to the Marxian dilemma. For the present purpose, we can break out of it by means of a theoretical device: we assume simply that labor productivity is a variable which is movable at will. We shall try to study what happens when (for whatever reason) it goes on increasing. We make the further initial assumption that the surplus created by more efficient habit is transferred and put into constructive use, nourishing such secondary social functions as are performed in vertically integrated cities by rulers, churches, courts, armies, educators, and so on. In a dynamic setting we are returned to problems already familiar in the static.

The ruler (without the instrumentality of which this movement of vertical integration could not take place) must be envisaged as acting in his own interest, according to rules already analyzed. Whatever the setting, surviving rulers must try to maximize transfer over the long period. In the formal sense, transfer can be considered the product of the number of contributors and the contribution of each. At first sight, maximum transfer would seem to result when the ruler tries to maximize both factors. Yet it was found that as they were interdependent, maximum transfer was attained before the point of maximum population possible at any moment. At each given level of habit there was an optimum density of population. Hence, in any given territory transfer cannot be increased by increasing the number of contributors beyond the optimum. But the situation naturally changes when we introduce territory itself as a variable in the problem. Surplus, then, becomes in part a function of territory.

The increase in the efficiency of habit creates movements in all the interconnected equilibria. It starts by increasing transferable surplus per capita. In a given territory resources available for rule grow larger; they permit a higher vertical integration by expansion and multiplication of the secondary functions. But the development of the arts and means of administration, education, communication, etc., makes it possible to govern constantly larger territorial units. Hence, the ruler has the possibility of expanding territory and thus, at given levels of habit, adding to his total transfer by increasing the number of contributors. But this, in turn, permits still higher vertical integration, and so on in a self-perpetuating process. Assuming full mobility of habit, this process would end only when a city had absorbed all available territory.

Hence, in a process of social growth horizontal and vertical expansion are related to habit, as well as related to each other. Horizontal expansion involves some increase in vertical integration and vice versa. While through the whole process the primary social functions retain their sway, there are added in a cumulative process secondary functions along the vertical axis peculiar to each stage of development. This represents, as it were, the qualitative aspect of social growth, and all change in quantity comes to imply some change in quality and vice versa. This simple relationship illustrates the danger of transposing without the aid of careful functional analysis experience obtained in a "primitive" society upon experience obtained in highly evolved and complex civilizations.

These relationships tend to throw some light upon the thorny questions pertaining to state and territory. For, to start with, a city would seem to be planted in a seemingly infinite expanse of nature. Territory would appear cheap and a ruler could, with Plato, choose the kind and extent of territory that he thought he needed. But with the progressive growth of more effective habit, territorial requirements increase, for they tend to become, in the last analysis, a function of the efficiency of habit. Hence, if in the process of growth a city should run into an area where territorial expansion becomes difficult, or impossible, it would also run into an area of increasing resistance to change. While this resistance is not absolute, it is severe and cumulative. It is strong enough to abolish the assumption that a city, considered under the aspect of growth, can be defined in terms of territorial configuration. To analyze these relationships more fully we have to consider not a closed city, but a society of cities, and thus the nature and function of war. Meanwhile it suffices to say that the belief in geographically delineated nations as bases of social life implies a belief in the desirability and the possibility of arresting the development of habit at some particular stage. At times the belief in the sanctity and inviolability of national territory has assumed the heat and violence of a major creed. This indicates that the rate of social change, in reality, has been so slow that it has become natural to identify the station reached with the final destination. Historically speaking, there is much to justify a provisional assumption of this character. For it should be realized, of course, that the assumption on which we proceed, the full mobility of habit, is an extreme one, telescoping long—and as yet partially potential—developments into a single picture. In reality, such mobility, though not hypothetical, is so opposed by numerous forces that it is often arrested. These opposing forces have now to be considered.

The technical facility of social growth depends, as we said, largely on the size of transferable surplus. While we seem unable to account for the rise of a first surplus in logically consistent terms, we do know something about the problems and difficulties connected with the later creation, collection, and use of such surplus. At most levels of experience, surplus represents a tiny fraction of the social product; it is still very small in most contemporary societies. And difficult as it is to create and scrape together, the risks of wastage are enormous. Rather than being piped into socially creative channels, it is generally wasted on the way by abortive population expansions, extravagant consumption, indecisive and prolonged wars, incompetent and luxurious rulers, and their retinues of wicked and slothful servants. And the lower the level of habit, the greater these risks seem to be. It is only after habit is well under way towards higher efficiency that societies seem to acquire a conscious habit of saving, investment, and the consistent care of the secondary functions. And it is only at such later stages that the initial and truly powerful resistances to technical change begin to decrease significantly. It is then only that society acquires any considerable margin of free choice. Indeed the larger the surplus becomes proportionately the smaller becomes the resistance to further change. The richer flow of surplus makes itself felt as a recession of necessity and the rise of human initiative. But whatever level habit may reach, surplus remains the lifeblood of social change. The danger of its being wasted assumes new forms and becomes, in a sense, more threatening than before. Men may overestimate their own freedom and, victims to new forms of hybris, imagine that human freedom is a matter of inherent right, rather than achievement built on continued expenditure of effort and restraint. For a waste of surplus—in unwise consumption, war, civil strife, excessive population expansions—that starves the secondary functions upon which rest levels of integration already achieved, leads first to the arrestment and later to the reversal of the process of social growth. And this danger is, in reality, so much the more vivid when at higher stages of habit the capital accumulation permits a period during which such waste can continue apparently unpunished. When the results become apparent, productivity has already fallen so low that the surplus required for the maintenance of the system cannot be produced and collected. After a point, therefore, the contraction process is rapid, resembling a debacle rather than an ordered retreat, and it becomes irreversible. The higher the previous degree of vertical integration, the more cataclysmic will the fall back towards nature appear, and the greater will be the number of people who must disappear before the rout can be stopped.

These are in drastically shortened perspective the external mechanisms of social growth and contraction. But, as we have already said, they are simple when compared with the inner, and more general, problems involved in any change of habit. We have indicated certain lines of development and certain conditions to which social growth has to submit. By means of a theoretical fiat, we let habit fluctuate at will. It is now time to let this assumption fall and consider habit change in its own context.

It was driven home to us in our wanderings in the cities of Plato and Aristotle that habit was protected by the double and combined might of obligation and belief. And, so far, we have found many convincing reasons why any city, once it has come into existence, should continue to exist; but we have found no reason at all why habit, in actuality, should change. The primary energies contained in instinct, and the power of distinguishing the relation between means and ends contained in reason were interlocked in covering systems of habit and belief. There is no force, within the system as hitherto conceived, that would either change habit or dissolve belief. Each system is closed, and taken, in its own terms, subject to dissolution but not to gradual change. In order, therefore, to account for the observed phenomena of structural change in society, a further assumption becomes necessary. Going behind the observed phenomenon of change we have to postulate a force which meets the requirements needed for dissolution and reintegration of established habit and myth. This force, then, is in terms of our previous analysis an extrasocial one. It does not reside in environment. It must be thought as belonging to man, who is the supplier of the events of which society is composed. Man seems, at times, to have become a truly social animal. He assumes with docility the role assigned to him by founders of states and legislators. He meekly obeys the ruler and follows faithfully the laws and regulations of the city. But this is an appearance; in some recess of his being he remains aloof. In the language of myth he remains a stranger in the city, and a sower of seeds which are of a potentiality both creative and destructive. He is a creature of imagination endowed with the gift of dreaming dreams and seeing visions. And this power of imagination, innovation, and invention, it seems, is that force which is needed to account for change in habit and myth, and for their reintegration. This force of creation, however it may be described by psychology, we summarize in the following under the term *genius,* which thus takes its place beside the forces of instinct and reason.

Much remains to be said before we are in a position to understand the function of the force of genius in society. But we cannot avoid a first observation. If social systems, as we hitherto have known them, were exposed to a common danger, that danger was change. It was difficult, indeed impossible, to see how an incipient disagreement between habit and belief could fail to end in social disintegration. Hence, any innovator in habit or belief will to any existing city present himself as a danger; he presents existing society with a "challenge." Unless some new way of integration can be found, the "challenger" is also the destroyer. It is, then, only "when an individual, or a minority, or a whole society replies to a challenge with a response" [2] of reintegration that a society, in the process of growth, can successfully negotiate the step from one level of habit and myth to another.

The concepts of "challenge" and "response," therefore, should refer to a special group of phenomena. The terms have a precise meaning. They should not be confused with the technical problems of balance and the natural conditions of human life. They come into play only when society is about to move from one kind of equilibrium to another. To understand the nature of man's creative potentiality becomes our next task.

[2] Arnold Toynbee, *A Study of History,* vol. III, p. 377.

7

Genius Visits

THE CITY

MAN AS HE ISSUED FROM THE HANDS OF NATURE WAS
A BEING WHO WAS BOTH INTELLIGENT AND SOCIAL.
. . . BUT THE INTELLECT, DILATING BY ITS OWN
EFFORTS, HAS ENTERED UPON AN UNEXPECTED
DEVELOPMENT. IT HAS LIBERATED HUMAN BEINGS
FROM SERVITUDES TO WHICH THEY HAD BECOME
CONDEMNED BY THE LIMITATIONS OF THEIR
NATURE. . . . THROUGH THE MEDIUM OF THESE
WILLS INSPIRED BY GENIUS, THE ÉLAN OF LIFE
THAT TRAVERSES MATTER OBTAINS FROM
MATTER FOR THE FUTURE OF THE HUMAN
SPECIES, PROMISES OF WHICH THERE COULD NOT
EVEN HAVE BEEN ANY QUESTION AT THE TIME
THE SPECIES FIRST TOOK SHAPE.—*Henri Bergson* [1]

ANY EVOLVED CITY must be thought of as having reached its present
level of integration only by having successfully passed through
a series of "challenges" and "responses." The force strong enough
to challenge, at each stage, the combined might of obligation and
belief, and strong enough to effect a new integration, we found
to be contained in man's imaginative and inventive powers—

[1] *The Two Sources of Morality and Religion*, pp. 180–181.

powers which we summarized under the term of genius. This force has now to be introduced into the apparently closed and self-contained system of the city. We approach for the first time the inner and essential problems of social growth. It would be surprising if our masters had failed to observe, and in some way account for, a social phenomenon of this magnitude. We ask, then, how they found a place for the seed of the Sower in the apparently sterile ground of the city.

We recall that Plato asked for a "revolution in the soul" in the perfect ruler. At the time we considered the perfect ruler as an ingenious theoretical device, permitting us to isolate and study certain aspects of social order and structure. But it is more than this: it is no simple expression of perfectionism, or a result of the master's ignorance of the practical affairs of men. For the "revolution in the soul," presupposed in the ruler, may now be characterized as the process through which man is liberated from the bondage of habit and myth and becomes a consecrated servant of social reason and strives to perfect the city through the activity of invention. Indeed, the perfect ruler becomes, as it were, an instrument of the force of genius, and by this device Plato succeeded in incorporating the principle of change (implicitly contained in all evolved cities) into his apparently static construction.

An understanding of this double aspect of the *Republic* is of great importance; and to render clear the use that Plato makes of it let us consider the famous image of the cave. This figure has been variously interpreted, but in elementary terms, it represents a city in which men are governed by habit and myth. The prisoners are chained to their particular functions in strange attitudes; what they observe on the wall, or field of intellectual vision, are the shadows, or myths, projected there by the rulers.

The prisoners are convinced that the shadows are the only reality; they feel that the cave is their true home. They have become so used to half life that they hate the mental effort of change; the city of the cave has become incapable of change by its own volition; it can come about only by some outside intervention. The prisoners have to be "released and disabused of their error" by some outside agent. But the journey from the dark cave into the sun of reality is a painful one, and the prisoners have to be prodded. "And if you assume that the ascent and the contemplation of the things above is the soul's ascension to the region of the intellect, you will not miss my surmise. . . . But God knows whether it is true. But, at any rate, my dream as it appears to me is that in the field of knowledge the last thing to be seen and hardly seen is the idea of good." [2] The idea of good, or social ends, contained in the second impulse that was noted in reason, is in the Republic already grasped by the ruler; and as he is also given absolute power, the Platonic city can become at once static in appearance and dynamic in implication. The revolutionary force of genius can, without inner contradiction, be presented under the mask of power and legality. While the ruler was, no doubt, the original revolutionary, and while this identification of genius with rule contains insight worthy of Plato, it is not in regal robes that genius usually discloses itself. We may be better served, therefore, by removing the mask of power from the face of genius, and study "some lofty soul born in a mean city." [3] Turning to Plato's master, Socrates, we encounter the archetype of the social inventor, as in the myth of Prometheus we meet the archetype of the technical inventor.

Socrates belonged to a city that had already created an intel-

2 *Republic,* 517b.   3 *Ibid.,* 496b.

lectual class which questioned habit and myth in search of new social ends. Socrates, though himself poor, had leisure for contemplation and meetings at the philosopher's corner, where ". . . young men of the richer classes, who have not much to do, come about me of their own accord; they like to hear the pretenders examined, and they often imitate me, and proceed to examine others." [4] But the rulers watching these meetings concluded: "Socrates is a doer of evil, who corrupts the youth; and who does not believe in the Gods of the State, but has other new divinities of his own." [5] This official attitude will be examined in due course; Socrates denied the charge, and set about explaining his mission.

But so strange was this mission, even in Socrates' own eyes, that he attributed it to a special "sign, a voice that comes to me." This voice, which he tells us was not previously heard in the city, compelled obedience. In Socrates' words: "I would rather die having spoken after my manner, than speak in your manner and live." [6] In trying to express more precisely what the voice wished him to accomplish he consciously engages in a rather clumsy image: "If I may use such a ludicrous figure of speech, [I] am a sort of gadfly, given to the state by God; and the state is a great and noble steed who is tardy in his motions owing to his very size, and requires to be stirred into life. I am that gadfly which God has attached to the state, and all day long and in all places, am always fastening upon you, arousing and persuading and reproaching you." [7] Socrates, guided by his daemon, tried to stir the city into life. He asked his fellow citizens to abandon their customary ways, to worship a new god, and to transform the known city into something as yet unknown. There is a par-

---

[4] *Apology,* 23c.   [5] *Ibid.,* 24b.   [6] *Ibid.,* 38e.   [7] *Ibid.,* 30e.

ticular quality to Socrates' prodding. The rulers—with that fine nose of theirs—almost at once smelled a secret power. Insignificant as Socrates may have appeared to an unwary beholder when he stood before the judges of the Athenians, his was a spark of creation. Much of his time was spent in liberating men from old bondage, and "there is irony running through Socrates' teaching." The spark of creation is not always apparent "and outbursts of lyricism are probably rare; but in the measure [that] these outbursts cleared the way for a new spirit, they have been decisive for the future of humanity." [8]

In the Socratic drama we watch the breakings of the molds of social predestination. Social theorists are constrained to deal with past genius, and their contribution, together with all other social data. But a contemporary theorist would have lacked the means of foreseeing Socrates' contributions; and to this day theory remains impotent to ensnare authentic genius in the meshes of *ex ante* analysis. We are in the position of a first observer watching the life of a plant from seed to seed. We would be less than men, if we did not marvel at what came to pass, and if we did not discard theories which had been formed on the basis of observations pertaining only to a part of the plant's cycle of life.

The endowment of genius we believe to be a gift of nature, for there is no reason to assume that the proportion of potential genius changes with time and place. Indeed, each human being may well be thought of as a potential inventor. But it can be observed that the proportion of operative genius does change; and we are justified in assuming that social conditions may be more or less favorable for its emergence and operation. We are unfortunately compelled to pass lightly over the most difficult question

[8] Bergson, *The Two Sources,* p. 55.

of all—how a first genius comes to emerge from the state of nature. The more "primitive" a society—the less vertical integration it has achieved—the greater is presumably the sway of habit and myth in it. By definition we have agreed that such sway is absolute in a state of nature. Education—most particularly in the wide sense of habituation—must aim at the mean; deviations from it not only lack incentive but arouse suspicion and outrage popular piety. But in order to emerge, a man pursued by genius must follow a different course; he must by his own effort evolve into what represents a new social species. He must leave the common road; he must alienate himself from the fellowship of man; like a criminal he must become a stranger in his native city. In the cold terms of probability, it does not appear likely that such a "heroic and divine kind of nature" will spontaneously grow out of a presocial ground. But, if we do not see our way to grant such a probability, there remains mythical intuition. For the hero "seemed not the child of mortal man, but of God." [9] And mankind has upon their early geniuses placed the cross of being sons of God.

The dilemma does not dissolve, but seems to become more acute if we inquire how historical genius appears on the scene: for those who are competent in their own right to discuss the matter seem to agree that genius does not generally emerge spontaneously, but that, when the time is ripe, it comes forth under the influence of preexisting genius, "like a light caught from a leaping flame; and once alight, it feeds on its own flame henceforward." [10] Leaving aside the unexplained question of the first emergence, genius spreads in the ordinary course of events through a kind of contagion. Experience suggests that

[9] *Iliad,* xxiv, lines 258 f.   [10] Plato's *Letters,* 341c.

authentic genius is rare, and its appearance unpredictable. "Nature's part," says the Philosopher, "evidently does not depend on us, but as a result of some divine causes is present in those who are truly fortunate; while argument and teaching, we may suspect, are not powerful with all men, but the soul of the student must first have been cultivated by means of habits for noble joy and noble hatred, like earth which is to nourish the seed. . . . The character then must somehow be there already with a kinship to virtue, loving what is noble and hating what is base."[11] Few men, either by nature or education, seem fit to receive and rekindle the "leaping flame" in its full splendor. But once kindled it does not burn in vain. The force of genius, like all other force, cannot come into being without effects, direct or indirect. In those who are "truly fortunate" the voice of genius finds an answer. The many may fear, and thus hate and persecute, genius, but in some it awakens echoes. Before the first voice is stilled the echoes set in motion affect men's opinions of themselves, their own lives, and the life of the city. There is a stirring in men's souls, and it will not be put down, particularly among the "young men of the richer classes who have not much to do."

This stirring of the soul is the effect of force, but becomes itself a force. While, at a price, it may be stilled by the city, it tends of its own accord to expand from the small, compact nucleus. To use the well-worn simile, like a stone thrown into the water, it causes rings to spread in widening circles. A new soul, kindled into flame, may break loose and set up new unrest around itself, and so on till the whole social surface is stirred by interlocking systems of unrest which try to combine into a new, as yet undefined, pattern.

[11] *Nicomachean Ethics,* 1179b.

We have observed such processes in many cities. But sometimes the stirrings have subsided, all seemingly returning to the old; sometimes they have led to violent destruction and social dissolution. Genius is a force, and the moving spirit may let loose the waiting monsters of chaos. In order to lead to life its force must become lawful, reconciled to what is possible and what is necessary. Even if a force is unpredictable, it must not be considered as arbitrary and magical. It is necessary, therefore, to examine how genius can be bent to perform the offices of construction rather than destruction. For even if social growth involves the destruction of one particular form of social balance, continued social life requires, as we have said, not the absence of all balance, but the re-creation of new balance.

Suppose, by way of illustration, that we are observers present when the city is first moved by the hope of a good life and new social ends in general. These ideas would be new to experience; they would herald a new life, a new order to be born. They would challenge experience—that safe ground of empirical science—and look for another ground in the future. Against the first voice of experience and piety they would raise the second voice of experiment and faith.

The system of myths is set to guard the outer social balance of society; but this balance is observable in the past only, and the projection point of myths must be thought of as located in the past. But the souls stirred by genius would start to breed all kinds of practical notions which would seek to influence men's actions and men's opinions about society. These practical notions, springing up in the city, would seek to perform much the same functions as myth. Indeed, for all practical purposes, they are projections in the inner kingdom, and in order to separate them from myth we shall call them *norms.* These norms are footless in past experience, and their projection point originally is located in the future, and supported by hope. It seems then that the idea of social growth gives birth to, and is unthinkable without, a double—mutually conflicting—system of myth and norm. Now recalling with what care the ruler must guard the purity of myth, we are thrown headlong into conflict; and the most vital questions of social life come to be contained in the encounter between myth and norm.

In order to illustrate further this encounter we shall use an image. Try to visualize the outer kingdom of a static city in the form of a vertical plane moving along a horizontal time-axis. In the past, or let us say to the left, we imagine the projection point of myth supporting the pattern of social events. The social plane or the outer kingdom may expand or contract, but the pattern of events itself retains its identity, like iron particles imprisoned in a magnetic field. This situation persists as long as it is not disturbed by a new force. At the moment when norm is born there springs up, as it were, a new projection point, not in the past, but in the future, to the right. The norms radiating from this point strike the social plane on the opposite side from myth. Hence norms affect social events; and the existing pattern is, so to speak, broken into; it dissolves into new configurations destroying the old social balance more or less completely, depending on the relative force of the two competing projection systems. And as the city cannot endure unless social balance is restored, the problem created by the stirring of genius is in the first place to find the means of incorporating myth and norm into a system which permits of social balance. As we consider here cases of social growth only, and not all the abortive attempts, it follows that the social balance sought must be different from anything previously experienced. The old outer social balance has ceased to be an infallible guide. We have arrived at a point where the social process begins to assume the character of a leap, and logic can only slowly catch up with the lightning movements of events. This is not peculiar to social theory; it occurs in nature whenever we watch the mutation of one kind of equilibrium into another. But the student is obliged to suspend judgment until he begins slowly to perceive the process as a whole.

The problem is not altogether new: it is in essence identical to that encountered by Aristotle in the determination of virtue. The philosopher was careful to teach us that the relationships between the outer and inner kingdoms were not simple. The two kingdoms were conceived as mutually interdependent, and they could be studied in their interrelationship or not at all. It is only after we have studied "what sorts of influence preserve and destroy states . . . [that] we shall perhaps be more likely to see with a comprehensive view . . . what laws and customs [we] must use." [12] And norm, as little as myth, can be determined by fancy and feeling alone; it needs the discipline of being constantly referred to the impartial judgment of social balance, for "the virtue of the citizen must . . . be relative to the constitution of which he is a member." [13]

Hence, if norm pretends to take over the function, no matter how partially, of myth, it must protect some social balance, and determine the form of the balance at which it aims. Myth went to this task simply: it aimed at protecting a system of habit which must be thought as historically given, and observable in reality. But norm has the ambition to change society into something

[12] *Nicomachean Ethics,* 1181b.   [13] *Politics,* 1276b.

new; it sets out into realms still unconquered by experience: but it cannot escape the objective necessities contained in the relationships of social balance. This places a new burden on the mind, and it would appear more safe to retreat to the valley of custom; but, says the Philosopher: "We must not follow those who advise us, being men, to think of human things, and, being mortal, of mortal things, but must, so far as we can, make ourselves immortal, and strain every nerve to live in accordance with the best thing in us; for even if it be small in bulk, much more does it in power and worth surpass everything." [14] Genius must cease to be a mere gadfly that God gave to the State; in a "comprehensive view" it must emerge above the valley of custom and, lacking experience, create in the mind a new city, a more perfect state, which must take the place of experience in the formation of norm.

Independently of each other founders of state have, faced with this great task, adopted a common method. The perfect cities they created, are far more than exercises in logic, or excursions into wishful thinking; they are parts of the social process of creation itself. If perfect cities forget that that is necessary, they become footless and dangerous. They must ever be geared to what is possible. Founders of state, indeed, have no other way than to build social models which incorporate into experience the new elements of norm. And in constructing such models experience has its place; "for the perfect state cannot exist without a due supply of the means of life. And therefore we must presuppose many purely imaginary conditions, but nothing impossible." [15] But nothing is impossible! And so before proceeding, Aristotle, as Plato before him, is led into the study of the social functions and the kinds of habit required for balance. For "as

[14] *Nicomachean Ethics,* 1177b-1178a.   [15] *Politics,* 1325b.

the weaver or shipbuilder or any other artisan must have the material proper for his work . . . so the statesman or legislator must also have the materials suited to him." [16] It is his task to find out a priori how the new element of norm can harmoniously—and without inadvertently causing social disintegration—be woven into a seamless social pattern.

But if the city is not to fall back into nature, it must during a period of transition be protected against premature change. Hence, the good citizen has a first duty; he must mold his character and guide his actions according to the particular social balance of his native city. But the "truly fortunate," the man aspiring to perfect virtue, becomes in addition a citizen of the inner kingdom of the perfect city. He acquires a double citizenship; he lives outwardly a good citizen of the visible city, while he inwardly has already taken up domicile in the invisible city of the future. He aims at molding thought, character, and action in its perfect forms; in the very effort he affects the social mass around him in subtle ways and in a common direction; his life becomes an example—a beacon on the way from mere life to good life, and men, and more particularly the leaders of men, have been for millennia inward members of the kingdoms we have now entered. Weakness and circumstance have let men fall short of the vision, but only ignorance would pretend that the West, for better or worse, would be what it has become, were it not for a common citizenship with great masters in perfect cities. What we have stumbled upon is not a common theoretical construction but, curiously, the integrating force of the city itself. "And this sort of thing," concludes Socrates, "is recollection and is most commonly a process of recovering that which has been forgotten through time and inattention." [17]

---

[16] *Ibid.*, 1325b-1326a.   [17] *Phaedo*, 73e.

8

Sacrifice

IN THE CITY

BECAUSE I HAD PITY FOR MAN, I MET
MYSELF NO PITY, BUT AM RUTHLESSLY
PUNISHED, A SIGHT THAT BRINGS SHAME
UPON GOD.—*Aeschylus* [1]

WHEN EARLY GENIUS STIRRED among the Hellenes we are told that "the gods, taking the disguise of strangers from other lands walk[ed] up and down the cities in all sorts of forms." [2] The strangers, sowed the seed, or "challenge," of social growth; but if an oracle had announced the power of this seed, it would not have been believed. On the other hand, the ruler would have seen the unrest that the strangers brought about; he would have noticed a spread of disbelief, a weakening of ancient piety, and a tangling up of the projections of myth. The confusion in the inner kingdom would represent a threat to order in the outer, and the guardians of the state would get busy trying to protect it against internal dissolution. But in order to understand the task awaiting them we must again penetrate into the inner kingdom.

Habit had its counterpart in obligation. And as all socially relevant habits hang together, lend each other mutual support,

---

[1] *Prometheus Vinctus,* lines 241–243.   [2] *Odyssey,* XVII, line 485.

and "form a solid block," so do supporting myths hang together, lend each other mutual support, and "form a solid block." And as particular habits are supported by particular obligations, so are particular myths supported by particular beliefs. And as particular habits and particular myths are strengthened by the totality of habit and myth, so are the particular obligations and the particular beliefs strengthened by the totality of obligation and the totality of belief. A disturbance in any habit is immediately opposed by the particular habit and myth, by the particular obligation and belief, but ultimately, and more powerfully, by the undivided blocks of habit and obligation, myth and belief. "Thus the sum total comes to the aid of its parts, and the general sentence 'do what duty bids,' triumphs over the hesitations we might feel in the presence of a single duty." [3] The voice of habit was the only thing that could rightly be called a pure "categorical imperative." Coming down originally from nature it calls man back from whence he came; it leads the race on the self-conscious road of survival and turns the mind away from change. It is the very opposite of the voice that came to Socrates and told him to choose death rather than to heed the voice of habit. It is indeed against this first voice that genius speaks in its own way.

The enormous pressure of habit becomes, as we have seen, supportable only by the counter pressure of myth which we called the shadow of man's intelligence and a tribute to reason. Myth is an ally to habit and turns men away from innovation. Social change presupposes a "challenge" breaking through this double and almost absolute inertia. But this inertia, because it is hostile to change, performs also a necessary service in all cities already evolved by preventing them from regressing and returning

[3] Bergson, *The Two Sources,* p. 3.

to nature. Considering the high price at which social growth has to be bought, it is natural that the guardians of order should try to protect the city against any force that would tend to remove the safeguards which stand between it and anarchy. Genius—the stranger in the city—represents a very grave threat to existing order and to the undisputed gains of the past.

In a city that has achieved outer and inner balance, any disturbance, wherever it occurs in the outer connected systems, reacts through the system as a whole: cumulative processes may start and lead to complete social disintegration. It is essential, therefore, to understand how a city can successfully "respond" to the "challenge" of genius, and in a kind of mutation restore the double balances on a higher level of integration. In order to grasp the risk involved in all change, we should analyze first the conditions of change in the two kingdoms, and their natural relationships.

Habit never loses a degree of plasticity. Natural environment contains, as we said, inevitable elements of the unforeseen, elements to which social balances must be able to respond as a matter of routine, or cities will perish. By a "habit of habit" men can to some extent adopt new codes of life and work; the gate to new habit is never quite closed. And so strong is the totality of obligation that it may absorb and protect a certain proportion of new habit. But the risk of damage is greater the greater and more sudden the change; still, in actual practice we have the right to count on a fairly substantial margin of possible change.

Change in habit is, at any rate, less dangerous to obligation than change in myth to belief. It was shown above that operative myth must masquerade as fact. But facts are conceived as unchangeable, and when myth assumes the status of fact, it becomes immutable. Myth is naturally static, and seems to be the rock upon which the city is founded; it remains vital as long as it meets the need of the ruler for obedience and the need of the subject for rationality. But when a habit changes, the particular myth that supports it will fail to meet these criteria: and it will cease to interpret experience meaningfully. When man loses belief in a particular myth, he is close to discovering the discrepancy between myth and fact; and sooner or later even the thoughtless, untroubled by the reserves of the wise, are sure to discover, alas, that myth is myth. Disbelief in one myth leads to disbelief in others and to a change in the spiritual climate. The explosion of myth becomes, in a climate of disbelief, the easy sport of vulgar minds: and it is only a matter of time before the totality of belief will evaporate. And the same sequence of events is as likely, or more likely, to be set in motion if the ruler follows the superficially rational course of modifying the projection of myth with change in external conditions.

Once the Stranger has succeeded in changing either habit or myth, a process would seem to have started which in time can dissolve the whole system of belief. If this process is not checked, the system of habit will lose all support from myth, and finally come to rest on force alone. This period during which the outer kingdom has to exist without support of an inner, we call *interregnum*—a special case of which has become known as the revolutionary dictatorship of the proletariat. But we have shown also that a city cannot exist very long if it is based on force alone, and fear becomes its chief or sole binding force. Overexpansion of the function of order would lead to retrogression, disintegration, and in the extreme case to a return to a state of nature. Social change can succeed only if we can prevent the rise of a prolonged socially

destructive interregnum. We must consider how it is possible
to change habit and myth without calling forth such a state.

Even in the best age of a civilization there remain areas of
disagreement between obligation and belief. These areas are centers of social unrest and the breeding grounds of monsters. Even
if the areas are small and the monsters still young, they represent an
actual and potential danger that has to be met by the use or display of force. It is, in a general theory, impossible to state how
large an expenditure on order a society can afford before social
balance becomes impossible. It depends on many circumstances
such as the size of the social surplus, the arts of government and
police. For short periods expansion of order can go further than
what is consistent with long-time balance; and a government may
meet a passing crisis with a temporary expansion of force without
lasting damage being necessarily inflicted. We are close to the
popular notion of order: we conceive might as the positive, variable instrument of government, and belief as a constant force
that ultimately keeps society together by preventing a runaway
expansion of order. The underlying relationships are not vitiated
by the fact that with an elastic use of force society may, within
limits, make up for variations in belief.

Nor do we overlook the persistency of a system of habit: the
"habit of habit" is elastic and tends to outwear myth. For a time
after the death of belief men live and act much as usual, driven
by the persistent sense of obligation. A well-timbered system of
habit can function on its own momentum. If a system of myth
and belief were suddenly to disappear in a city, a casual visitor
would probably fail to notice anything amiss. Some inhabitants,
even among the cultured, might tell him that the death of the gods
was a good thing. They would point with pride to the prosperous

condition of finances and to rich productions in the fields of art and literature as proofs that men can get along without outworn superstition; they would say, perhaps, that men were at last free and had come into their own. In this city of man, culture would, for all we know, reach that kind of late flowering that attracts amateurs of corruption.

We may count, therefore, on a period of grace during which society is carried along by the momentum of habit; this period may in theory be used to establish a new system of myth. But such a creation must be completed before the growth of the freed monsters has, through overexpansion of the function of order, led to disintegration. A successful "response" to a "challenge" presupposes the constitution of a new inner kingdom in time to prevent a prolonged interregnum. In the ideal case the interregnal period should be so brief as to be hardly noticeable.

We visualized the city in the likeness of a vertical plane proceeding along the time-axis. The projection point of myth was situated in a past outer social balance; the projection point of norm "challenging" it, was an imagined social balance in the future. Myth rationalized and made supportable present habit; norm supported and made desirable a new set of habits. But we said, too, that in order to be socially significant the system of norm must contain nothing impossible; in other words, once such a new system of habit has become realized it must become stable and self-perpetuating on a higher level of integration. We may visualize, therefore, the interregnal point as that in which the social plane passes the norm-projection point and leaves it behind. This passage is achieved when habit is changed to agree with new norms; and this holds true even if change in habit represents only a compromise between the old and the new. To an observer on the social plane, the norm projection point will henceforward approach closer and closer to the myth projection point until both, at a sufficient distance, become indistinguishable. How, then, we ask, can this movement be achieved without bringing about a prolonged interregnum?

The solution is simple. Homer told us that genius takes on "the disguise of strangers." And have we not ourselves time and time again found that myth must masquerade as fact? And for the same reason that myth had to be disguised in the first place, norm must, in its turn, take up the mask and become to all appearances a myth. For if, by some optical illusion, men could be tricked into believing that norms are myths (and thus made to anticipate what would be the real situation once a higher level of integration was achieved), much trouble and many a serious crisis could be avoided. The norm would, so to speak, slink unnoticed into the system of myth and would profit from the totality of belief rather than destroy it and so in the last instance destroy itself. It is then for some such process by which norm may be transformed into myth that we must look.

Let us imagine that we are in the position of Plato's philosopher who by an act of fate has become a ruler. If we had been ordinary men,—unconscious of social ends and the law of reason governing ends-means relationships,—we would have tried brutally to change existing habit by mere command and the use of force. But we would then have destroyed totality of belief, and in the ensuing interregnum—which obviously must be a long one, as it takes generations to re-create belief—the habit system which we were trying to impose would also be destroyed. But as philosophers, would we not, before we acted at all, try to understand and later utilize existing myth and belief? It seems, therefore, that a philosopher—as opposed to a man who is merely cultured in the sense of a particular city—would not succumb to the temptation of exposing and destroying myth, and thus the slowly built up totality of belief. It seems certain, too, that he would by some means gain control over existing myths—not in order to expose them but in order to make them subservient to his new norms. We fancy that a philosopher in such a situation would begin by inventing tales, telling the subjects that the myths are parts of divine truth; and he would show them the outward respect due to truths of high origin. But this would only be half of the tale. He would find some fiction—which in the metaphysical sense may be either true or false—by means of which he could implant the idea that divine order, though once and for all given, was only slowly and gradually imparted to man, and first to the rulers. The philosophers he might proselyte with the notion that the discernment of these preexisting ideas is the work of enlightened reason. But the realm of ideas is, on the whole, too bloodless to appeal to the multitude, which rather seems to ask for signs and miracles. Subjected to the categorical imperative, it is not prepared to listen to a Socratic daemon—which is still the lonely property of genius—unless it is reduced to a visible manifestation. In ages when gods walk up and down the cities, divine revelation is to the multitude a final authority; it is received with the uncritical acceptance that meets a scientific revelation in ages when science has assumed the miracle-working function. The philosopher, therefore, would surely tell the multitude that he has established monopolistic communication with the divine. This fiction could take many forms; the channel of communication may be a returned traveler from the other world, like Er; the messenger may be a stranger, the son of a mortal mother and an

immortal god; the ruler may, like Moses, claim to have received
a divine command; and finally the ruler, or the aspiring ruler,
may become a "scientist" pretending to have discovered the "laws"
of society and the dark ways of historical necessity. In reality, we
find that all these philosophical devices have been used to conquer
for rulers the necessary control over the mythical.

In a state of nature the inner kingdom would, like the others,
be mainly on the horizontal model. The individual's reason would
be satisfied by the interposition of a number of disconnected
functional deities, or acting forces. Integration between them
would be rudimentary. But if the city is to rise vertically, the
inner kingdom must, at each successive step, support the new
outer integration by a corresponding inner integration. And if this
be so, we must conclude that all myths supporting vertical integration above such a natural minimum have once begun their
careers as norms and in the course of time become indistinguishable from myth. Even if myth and norm from the beginning
are enemies, they have been made at times to lie down together,
and more, to appear to the observer as of one nature, the norm
chameleon-like indistinguishable from myth.

Hence norm should, as near as possible to the point of emergence, be projected back in such a way that it will appear as
radiating from the existing myth projection point. It must don the
authoritative cloak of myth; and the subjects must, by some
optical trick, be made to perceive the city as having already passed
the still future projection point of norm and thus already reached
the point where norm and myth of their own accord appear as one.
Consequently, the wise ruler would tell his subjects that norm is
not norm at all, that it is myth and as myth fact, eternal and
changeless. Any lack of belief in the now disguised norm would

be explained by former blindness and a vulgar lack of perception. Hence, the outer reform, about to take place, would be preceded by a reform in the inner kingdom, masquerading as a new revelation of long-past events. And turning to realities we find that, each time that the cities prepare to mount the ladder of vertical integration, they return, or so they say, to the primordial sources of their myths and religions. For in the inner kingdom the apparent step backward seems needed for the spring of a forward leap.

The social functions are universal; what primarily (but not exclusively) changes in higher integration are the habits of order. Thus, it is to be expected that the reform in the inner kingdom will chiefly concern the hierarchy of the gods. The deities of production, reproduction, and war, however they have been arranged to meet shifting conditions and fancies, will have their place in the new construction; they should not be destroyed; what is needed are deities which reflect the need for new order. It would carry us beyond our scope to enter into a discussion of this process; let it be enough to say that there will emerge gods who lord it over the others, that we shall witness the beginning of the domination of Zeus and Odin. And because the old gods continue to live, the new god can take over their authority and strengthen it; the new god can inherit the belief in the old and rejuvenate it. For if such a reform is carried through with wisdom and without unseemly haste, the illusion of an undivided static inner kingdom need not be shaken. Norm can masquerade as myth, and both as fact. Totality of belief would remain to steady the city in its leap over the abyss of interregnum from an old to a new equilibrium. In reality, of course, we do not expect theoretical perfection. Totality of belief may be hurt in many ways: there would be experimentation, abortive attempts, confusion, and delay. But the expansion of force in government may temporarily carry the city; and delays and frictions are not necessarily fatal.

And returning to the *Republic* we find in it, not unexpectedly, an almost perfect illustration of the processes which we theoretically deduced. We noted in it previous, implicit historical change; but now, considering it in its own setting of time and place, we note that in all particulars it meets the requirements it would have to meet as a "response" to a Socratic "challenge." But so quietly has the Master gone to the task and so skillfully are norm and myth blended together that many wise and learned commentators have found it difficult to decide where the one ends and the other begins. Or rather, most later philosophers have failed altogether to note the dynamic implications of the *Republic,* deceived by its majestically static appearance; and indeed this is the highest tribute possible to Plato's incomparable mastery of the inner kingdoms. The deception was facilitated by the fact that in the *Republic* the genius was also the ruler; the great social mutation, implicit in the Platonic scheme, could in theory take place with a minimum of violence and a minimum of friction.

But in real cities, the genius is wont to take up the disguise of a stranger. He remains unpredictable; he blurts out to all comers what the daemon prompts him to say. Unlike the Master he seems often to lack the inclination and the skill required for the manipulation of the inner symbols in the oblique manner. And to all appearances the stranger babbling at the philosophers' corner is not fit to be the companion of the immortal gods. Indeed, we may even be censored by some pedagogue if we tell him that the stranger is a son of God. Nor could we deny that the rulers, the high priests, and all the guardians of order are justified in considering such a stranger as the herald of interregnum. Whatever his virtue as a man, the guardian is bound to let one man die rather than to permit the city to be thrown into anarchy. And if the stranger stirs up the city, it is meet that he be sacrificed. We have by simple logic reached a first great mystery in the city; logic is joined by history in telling us over and over again of this sort of sacrifice, which remains close to the heart of myth and religion.

But if the seed has taken root, it will, dying, give new life and the city cannot return to the old. The stranger, laying down what is accidental, takes a place among the creators, the gods of the city, whom the rulers must honor henceforward in order to secure their own rule. The full power of genius is revealed only after death; resurrection is part of its destiny, and the strangers ask that we spare them our pity: "And so, my judges, you must be of good cheer about death, must recognize the truth of this one thing, that no evil at all befalls a good man while he lives or after he has died, nor are the gods neglectful of his affairs. It is not by chance that what has happened to me now has happened; on the contrary, it is clear to me that it was better that I die now and be quit of the business of life. This is the reason why the Sign nowhere turned me aside, and this is the reason why I am not very angry with those who voted to condemn me, or with my accusers. And yet it was not with the expectation of conferring a benefit upon me that they voted for my condemnation, that they brought their accusations against me, but because they thought to harm me. And for this they are blameworthy." [4]

We set out to build the city with a single purpose—life. And now in order that the city may come into being and continue to live, men have to seek the good life; and in order that the city

[4] Plato, *Apology,* 41c-d.

shall gain its life, some men, or so it would seem, must give their
own. Like Prometheus, they must be sacrificed and their sweet
and stormy souls return to a home

> Where never creeps a cloud, or moves a wind,
> Nor ever falls the least white star of snow,
> Nor sound of human sorrow mounts to mar
> Their sacred, everlasting calm. . . .

9

THE CITY
Goes to War

IT IS OFTEN ASKED AS A MIGHTY OBJECTION, WHERE
ARE, OR EVER WERE, THERE ANY MEN IN SUCH
A STATE OF NATURE? TO WHICH IT MAY SUFFICE
AS AN ANSWER AT PRESENT, THAT SINCE ALL
PRINCES AND RULERS OF "INDEPENDENT" GOVERN-
MENTS ALL THROUGH THE WORLD ARE IN A
STATE OF NATURE, IT IS PLAIN THAT THE WORLD
NEVER WAS, NOR NEVER WILL BE WITHOUT
NUMBERS OF MEN IN THAT STATE. . . . IT IS NOT
EVERY COMPACT THAT PUTS AN END TO THE
STATE OF NATURE BETWEEN MEN, BUT ONLY THIS
ONE OF AGREEING TOGETHER MUTUALLY TO
ENTER INTO ONE COMMUNITY, AND MAKE ONE
BODY POLITIC; OTHER PROMISES AND COMPACTS MEN
MAY MAKE ONE ANOTHER, AND YET STILL BE
IN THE STATE OF NATURE.—*John Locke* [1]

THE FIRST FOUR CHAPTERS of this book examined the nature of
a static society; the following four examined conditions of social
change. We move from the problems of structure to those of
process. In both cases we deal with a closed, isolated city, but

[1] *Of Civil Government,* book II, chap. 2.

in real life, cities exist in systems of interconnected states. Such a system generates forces, and exhibits phenomena, which are absent in the closed city, and the next stage of the inquiry, therefore, is to study the impact of such systems upon social events. While defense was from the outset included among the primary social functions, the "need" for defense in the closed city was equal to zero and could not exert any weight in the social balance. But in a political universe—a system of militarily or politically interconnected cities—defense has to be given determinate positive values within each state. The determination of these values is the starting point for the present departure.

Growth of cities was indistinguishable from changes in territorial requirements. Hence, several cities—one of which at least is in a process of growth—will sooner or later meet and come into contact and thus form a political universe. Consider a small model universe composed of two cities which at first are equal in all respects.

In each city the functions of production, reproduction, and order are determined by domestic needs. Defense, on the other hand, is determined, not by such needs, but by the power of the defense function in the neighboring state. In other words, the function of defense is a result of the configuration of force in the universe as a whole: it is determinate, not in domestic, but in universal terms. These relationships are basically simple, but they are decisive for the life of cities which can achieve social balance only if the "need" of defense, assigned to them from the outside, can be satisfied with internally given resources. If this "need" should be larger than can be met within this framework, cities either succumb in war, or already in "peace" consume in preparation for war, first, the social surplus and later the social substance. Hence, a stable, interstate equilibrium in the political universe is possible only so long as the habits in each city are just efficient enough to permit it neither to conquer nor to administer a territory larger than it already has; and thus defense is "cheap" enough to be financed within the limits of available surplus.

If their habits—more particularly those of war and administration—should become more efficient and both cities should attain the ability to exercise effective military and political action in the universe as a whole, the "need" for defense increases in both cities. This increase—unless interrupted by the outbreak of war—would be cumulative and thus break the bounds of any social equilibrium. For each time one city increased its armaments, the other would have to catch up and so forth. The armament race would use up the social surplus, and gradually absorb resources needed for other social functions. Both cities would be threatened by social contraction: it would be in the interest of both, and in that of the universe as a whole, that war should occur before—at least for one state—contraction sets in. The conquest of one city by the other offers a chance of survival, while a continued armament race is surely fatal to both. A unification of the two cities, even if by conquest, may lead to a restoration of balance and a continued life: for conquest leads to a total elimination of the external defense function.

Assume now that one city is twice as large and populous as the other. The relative surplus being the same, the "need" for defense would, in relative terms, be twice as large in the smaller city. The larger city could mobilize equal force with half the relative effort; and stopping short in the armament race before the social surplus was exhausted, it could force the smaller city beyond this point. And the greater a city is in relation to another,

the greater is, *ceteris paribus,* its relative advantage. Also the more
unstable does the equilibrium of the universe become: and provided that the efficiency of habit is not affected, each disturbance
in the universe tends to move it towards the underlying more
stable equilibrium by elimination of the smaller state, thus elimi-
nating the defense-function itself. Considering only this simplest
of cases it would seem that the equilibrium in a political universe
is so exceedingly unstable that unification through war is not only
inevitable, but also quick of accomplishment, particularly as the
process of unification left to itself tends to accelerate as it proceeds.
But this conclusion is premature; it fails to consider the wide-
spread social reactions to transfer of resources to defense from
other functions. These reactions are often violent, and they explain
not only the slow and uneven fusion of actual universes, but also
the reverse process of parcellation.

Rulers assign high priority to defense; war represents a dramatic
and total danger to the state; neglect of other social functions is
slower and more insidious in its effects. Hence, faced with foreign
enemies, rulers tend to transfer as much resources to defense as
they can. And as social resources are limited, they will first cease
to support such activities as seem to them the least essential for
immediate survival. Citizens will be trained in manly virtues—
blind obedience, courage, and disregard of life and property; there
will be need for soldiers and Mars will enter into union with
Venus. There will be little energy left to devote to production and
administration, and still less to the improvements of the arts. The
pressure of the defense function prevents, then, the increase of productivity and thus of transferable surplus. Indeed, by swallowing
up surplus, defense limits and circumscribes the process of social
growth already studied; it indirectly limits the "need" for, and

the potentiality of territorial expansion. As long as cities transfer just enough resources to defense, they stabilize prevailing habits and with it the extent of the territory that can be administered as one unit. It is often overlooked how slender the social surplus really is especially in the "primitive" societies. A very modest military establishment may easily absorb all of it; the pressure of the expansive defense function itself would therefore indirectly cut off the potentiality of social growth, and with it the possibility for any of a number of contending states and tribes to overcome the others. A relatively stable political universe can thus be bought at the expense of social development, and there may be underlying truth in the old maxim: if you want peace, prepare for war.

There is much that argues for the conclusion that such was generally the situation in early stages of social development. And if territorial expansion is not possible without previous social growth, requiring in its turn previous surplus, we arrive at the perhaps paradoxical conclusion that to break this impasse it is necessary that the pressure of defense on surplus should have decreased at some point and time. To consider these relationships we now turn to a political universe composed, not of two, but of several states.

In a system of hostile states it seems dangerous and difficult to decrease defense; it upsets the equilibrium between states and invites foreign plunder and destruction, if not conquest. But while such a lessening of the pressure of defense is difficult and dangerous, it is not temporarily impossible. Human life adapts itself slowly to changed circumstance, and there is room for the unexpected and the unlikely. We can imagine several ways by which this result can be achieved but consider here, by way of illustration, one only. The military pressure is, on the whole, less on the periphery than in the center of a political universe. The advantages of the peripheral position are unusually great when a country is separated from others by distance and natural obstacles; the sea has during long periods constituted such a barrier and it has generally been cheaper to maintain a navy than an army. It would be natural for a long "peace" to induce in some relatively favored city a feeling of security and make the citizens impatient with the Spartan mode of life. They may begin to limit expenditure on defense: private men can enjoy more luxury and leisure; some may even turn to intellectual pursuits; inventors may arise, change habit, and start a new cycle of social growth. With the increase in productivity social surplus would grow absolutely and relatively. This peaceful city would, after a while, have accumulated a greater surplus than its "better prepared" neighbors, and thus a greater military potential. In other words, as military potential is a function, not only of territory and population but also of the development of productivity, a state can compensate its numerical inferiority with technical superiority.

And it is for this reason that superiority, in the long run, tends to gravitate to countries which in "peace" were able to channel most social surplus into uses productive of social growth. A great peacetime establishment for war, by decreasing potential of growth, in the long run decreases relative military potential. But even so, the mobilization of this potential requires time; and it requires social mobility. How small a peacetime military establishment can safely be made depends on several factors: geographical configurations, relative size of states, development of habit, natural resources, and so on. A wise ruler will aim at keeping peacetime expenditure on defense at the minimum consistent with safety; he will find the means of shortening the period of mobilization, and prolonging the time available for it by means of alliances and diplomacy. In short, he will avoid the Scylla of overpreparedness and the Charybdis of underpreparedness. And the further civilization develops the more weight it will attach to the wise use of the social surplus in time of "peace," and the less upon the continuous expenditure upon armament. It is easy to understand why lasting dominion and conquest have tended to gravitate in actuality—not to nations which have organized themselves on a permanent military basis—but to nations which have developed the solid bases of productive superiority in time of "peace."

But the continuous rise in productivity and the ever more efficient habits of war which result from it are not without some further repercussions. Projecting this line of development onto the screen of the future it may be imagined that destructive techniques finally become so perfected that war, in addition to being fratricidal, becomes also suicidal. Little need be said about the potentialities of such black magic. In the annihilation of mankind social theory would be lost in the metaphysical. But social theory is directly concerned with the more present danger of the anticipation in people's mind of the ever-increasing destructiveness of war. In a senseless search for "security," preparations for defense may then absorb, not only available surplus, but go further, and even in time of "peace" set in motion irreversible processes of social contraction. The maintenance of highly developed social systems—capable of global wars of annihilation—require an abundant flow of surplus into channels always wider and more complex. If surplus, in a final panic, is drained into the nonproductive uses of defense, the efficiency of the system begins to decline, first slowly, and then at an ever-increasing pace. Surplus will contract, after a point, to such an extent that sufficient resources will not be forthcoming for the restoration of the system. The point beyond which recuperation becomes impossible and society lost in a mess of circular bottlenecks cannot be predicted a priori. But at some stage the system called forth by the life-giving properties of abundant surplus will begin to crumble. Finally, cities will begin to contract—vertically and horizontally—and return to more "primitive" levels of integration: the previous process of social expansion will be followed by the corresponding (and ever cataclysmic) process of contraction. Hence, the growth of productivity presenting men with the alternatives of social growth and war, may after a period tend to reverse itself and to become abortive. War then loses its powers of restoring universal balance. But at this point the defense-function will (if war has not previously been released) begin to contract. A kind of equilibrium may finally be reached by a general retreat to more "primitive" conditions—at the cost of giving up all the previous gains of social growth.

The risk of self-destruction through war, be it achieved directly or indirectly, is then proportionate to the height of the technical civilization: the risk increases as the political universes increase (for their previous unification has implied increasing productivity). The maximum of risk materializes when technical habits have reached the perfection required for global unification. But the cumulative list of risks consequent upon social growth is not at an end. When cities first emerge it must be assumed that they are small, and that habits, if not identical, are nevertheless similar in nature. In such a situation we found that wars would be long and bitter, though interspaced with temporary equilibria. Yet social growth is almost certain to involve diversification; and gradually one expects that the participating cities will show greater differences also in habit and efficiency in war. For a while wars would then tend to become shorter and less bloody. A strong victorious power could afford certain restraints, and in its own interest protect the vanquished. But still later the situation would change. War is a powerful agent of cultural diffusion. Cities incapable or unwilling to adopt the more efficient methods of production and destruction are the first to be knocked out and absorbed by more "progressive" nations. We expect, therefore, that in the final rounds the contenders will again be more evenly matched. These final wars will proceed on higher levels of efficiency and risk, and resume the protracted and unrestrained character of early wars of annihilation. This return to barbarism, intensifying the risk of total debacle, heralds the "time of troubles." The term is the prophet Daniel's but has been given new content by Arnold Toynbee.

So far we have considered a single political universe; but just as we imagine that many cities emerged out of nature, so we should imagine that several universes also emerged. In the beginning these grew independently of each other; later they came into contact, began to overlap and coalesce. In the course of history, centers of dead, or dying, universes survive as states; these are under the form of alliances and spheres of influence combining into new larger universes and so on. Some universes may even have lacked the time to coalesce into states before they were absorbed by another more expansive universe, or divided between several. And even when an obsolete universe *de facto* is absorbed by another, it may, like a small fish swallowed by a larger, continue its own internal motions for a while. These interminglings of patterns, these superimposed systems of movement, offer interesting problems; but theoretically they interest us because they explain how new units are fed into an expanding pattern of power; a process tending, on the whole, to slow down reactions previously observed in a single universe.

The political and military game in a universe has to be played in different ways according to the number and relative strength of the participating gamblers. But in all cases each participant finds it to his own survival interest to prevent, if he can, other states from increasing in relative power. And as long as the players are numerous and fairly evenly matched, a balance of power may be maintained in the universe for quite a while. The players adopt flexible systems of alliances, spheres of influence, annexations, and divisions. There develop apparent "rules of the game." Each player tries to prevent another from gaining an advantage unless he himself gains a corresponding one: the jealousy of all tends to mobilize enough force to maintain existing balance. As long as habit is fairly stable, such a game has chances of some success; it creates a certain semblence of international habit and almost morality; the major players seem to impose certain restraints upon themselves and may for a time avoid unlimited armament races and even maintain the fictions of "international law."

But such a system of habit requires conditions in each country which are either static, or changing at an equal rate; neither condition is likely to last long. If, for instance, one city should show a more rapid development of productivity, it would also (quite innocently) increase its relative military potential; other players would begin to get restive looking for compensation. One or the other would discover an increased "need" for defense. This, or some other reflection, would soon start a competitive increase in armaments, each city feeling itself hemmed in by compelling necessities. The cumulative increase in "need" for armaments influences the universe in several ways. The small cities are the first to feel the pressure of defense. They cease to be independent players; they either seek the protection of larger states, or try precariously to exist as "neutrals" in the vacua created in intersections of political tensions. In either case they have become merely pawns in the game. War is most likely to be released just before a major player approaches the point of social contraction, the point after which he would, in any case, be automatically eliminated from the game: the likely "aggressor" has, thus, the choice between peaceful elimination or the chances of war. In the ensuing war one or the other combination of powers will be victorious, and the number of effective players will be decreased. Hence, after a succession of conflicts there are fewer players and thus fewer possible power-combinations. In the later stages of the game the pretense of a balance of power has to be abandoned in naked striving for predominance of power. This general process can, as just said, to some extent be delayed by the fusion of several universes. When increases in productivity are large, the influx of new universes may compensate for the elimination of earlier players, and the game of balance of power—which prevents the defense function from exercising its full pressure—may be considerably prolonged. But the possibilities are gradually exhausted as we approach the single universe. The game can prolong the disunity of the whole universe and various circumstances can delay, but not prevent, a final unification—or disintegration of civilization.

War, therefore, is, as we have said, no accidental phenomenon in the life of man. To each participant war must present itself as objectively given by the struggle for social survival. Theory has no need, as it has no right, to explain the universal phenomenon of war by vague references to human nature or to lists of "causes" drawn from the arsenal of individual psychology. War like death is popularly ascribed to an infinite number of "causes." It is said that drowning, hanging, or old age are "causes" of death; but if we escape one such "cause," we are sure to fall victim to another. The ills by which we die cannot, therefore, be accepted as the final "cause" of death. In fact, a biologist would rather study the life process itself; he may come to visualize the organism in forms of an equilibrium which under the impact of alternative (but unavoidable) shocks sooner or later is bound to dissolve. The apparent "cause" of death would be a fortuitous circumstance, but necessity of death would rest in the nature of life itself. And as in life we are in death, so in peace we are in war. The factor releasing a war may be the ambition of a tyrant, the greed of an oligarch, the fanaticism of a partisan, the hysteria of the multitude. But in order to understand the persistency and necessity of war under so many forms and in so many ages, it is necessary to understand the nature of cities and systems of cities. Periods of "peace" may perhaps be prolonged by the removal of some occasions for war; but to abolish war more drastic changes are needed.

War, in the social sense, is the response to a disequilibrium caused by the peculiar and limitlessly expansive nature of the defense function. It is also directly related to the process of social growth. In its blind way war strikes at the root of the evil: it tends towards the final elimination of the defense function itself; it tends towards the unification of political universes and also towards safeguarding the possibility of social growth. Wars are the birth pangs—however often they lead to stillbirth—of universal states. They can be likened to fevers: while threatening the body with destruction they try to rid it of the cause of its disorder.

Hence, human behavior (and other alleged "causes" of war) are as much the effects of wars as their "causes." The particular cities are instruments of social growth and represent alternatives to anarchy or a state of nature. The true dilemma is caused by the fact that in performing their own functions they render themselves obsolete. On the levels upon which they emerge and operate self-consciousness necessarily screens the further truth that not death but the striving for isolated life is the enemy of growing life. The same deep currents which carried the city out of nature and let it grow, compel the city to train its citizens for war. The more a city grows the more precious and more unique does its own culture appear to it. The more terrible also appears the threat of conquest. Culture itself becomes an incitement to the training in warlike habits, to the propagation of warlike myth and, in fine, to the glorification of warlike characters. The further the process of social growth has been permitted to proceed, the greater becomes the necessity to inflame the particularist passions and strengthen the loyalties of men to their particular spot of an obsolescent system. And as long as the motive power of the cities is identified with the survival-interest, not of the universe as a whole, but with that of its component parts, so long is it foolish to discuss the means of "preventing" war. Indeed, the better nations get to understand each other, and the common necessities which govern the actions of each, the more reason do they have for fearing each other. The stronger becomes also that voice of prudence that warns them to play well the mortal game to which they have been called.

Presiding over the founding of the city we encountered the conflict between private and public interest; we have now encountered a not less mortal conflict between national and universal interest. Both cannot prevail. The alternative to war—if there be any—requires that we teach ourselves and then others to live according to universal loyalty. This conversion, if at all possible, is a slow, complex, and painful process. And the leap from the particular to the universal is not without risk. Existing cities would rightly see in the universal man their own death warrant, and may not welcome him. Still, the leap—or so the Universal Ruler tells us—is not without reward. For, "nothing is so conducive to greatness of mind as the power of systematically and truthfully testing everything that affects our life . . . to infer . . . its relation and value to the universe, and particularly to man as a citizen and member of that supreme world-city, of which all other cities form, as it were, households." [2]

[2] Marcus Aurelius, *To Himself,* III, II.

10

THE CITY
Conquers the World

> FOR MOST OF THESE MILITARY STATES ARE SAFE
> ONLY WHILE THEY ARE AT WAR, BUT FALL WHEN
> THEY HAVE ACQUIRED THEIR EMPIRE; LIKE UN-
> USED IRON THEY LOSE THEIR TEMPER IN TIME OF
> PEACE. AND FOR THIS THE LEGISLATOR IS TO
> BLAME, HE NEVER HAVING TAUGHT THEM HOW
> TO LEAD THE LIFE OF PEACE.—*Aristotle* [1]

WHENEVER CITIES BEGIN TO GROW, and "exceed the limits of necessity . . . a slice of [their] neighbor's land will be wanted . . .
and so [they will] go to war"; [2] and so on, until it is seen that
continuous social growth contains, as its own implicit end, the
global state. Social theory—lacking relevant experience—is unable to give a measured estimate of the risks which one city—
out-distancing all others—would have to run in order to reach
that final end. But we know that the process of unification through
conquest is so complex and so dangerous, that it may well end
in social disintegration. Nevertheless, giving the city the benefit
of the doubt, let it be assumed that after a "time of troubles" the
whole world becomes united under one ruler. Then, one might
perhaps hope that the ship of state would at last be safe. But un-

[1] *Politics*, 1334a.　　　　[2] *Republic*, 373b-e.

fortunately, the "response" to a universal "challenge" is not simple.

The founder of a first city could deal with an unformed mass of families in a state of nature. The founder of the universal state has to use the particularist remnants of preexisting cities. He has to contend with systems of long-developed habit and belief; he also inherits resentment, frustration, and fear among the vanquished; greed, arrogance, and pride among the victors. At the moment of fusion he could hardly prevent the victorious legions from indulging in plunder and spoliation: treasure and slaves would take the usual road to the victorious capital. The soldiery would expect their recompense. There would be an initial burst of excess and expense. Still, lasting government is not possible by squandering accumulated treasure. The ruler must consolidate the universal budget. The universe requires high productivity, surplus, and transfer in order to support an immense vertical superstructure. True, there might be savings on defense, but the legions must be kept in good temper by donations and bonuses; there must be set up a huge administration and police force; the ruler himself should shine in splendor seemly to the purple. And during the long war years he had surely told his own people that after victory their enemies would be punished and made to pay for the war. Perhaps, therefore, his people expect some alleviation in wartime taxes and levies. The ruler—meeting all these demands upon his treasury—would wish to place the burden on the conquered provinces.

Taxes come finally out of surplus which is determined by the efficiency of habit systems as a whole. The more highly evolved and the more productive a system becomes, the more dependent it is upon the integrated activities of many specialized skilled groups and the use of many initially expensive tools. These groups

—philosophers, priests, civil servants, educators, engineers, etc.—are nourished out of the social surplus; and increased taxation decreases the resources available for their use. The same applies to the savings needed to construct and maintain capital-equipment. The effect of increased transfer in provinces already exhausted by war, occupation, and plunder is to dissolve the skilled groups and to let capital run down. Transfer becomes self-defeating by drying up the sources of surplus; for the cost of maintaining the productivity of a system as a whole represents, as it were, a first mortgage on the surplus. If the ruler persists in taxing the provinces too heavily, the income from them continues to contract, and he has on his hands a process of social contraction which, if not quickly stopped and reversed, leaves him without the revenue required to master a global state; he would bring about a process of parcellation. In surviving universes—and we do not consider here all the abortive attempts—a ruler must soon impose restraints upon himself in dealing with the former enemy and some severity in dealing with his own people. Indeed, the greater, the richer, and the more populous the latter is when compared with the universe as a whole, the more must he depend upon continuous transfer from it.

There is no particular reason to imagine that the universal ruler is in love with justice; but if he is to found a lasting empire and thus fall under our preview, he has to oppose the ruling element in his own city and within given limits support the corresponding element in the conquered cities. Self-interest forces upon him the universal view—just as previously self-interest had forced upon him the national view. He must try to behave as if he were indeed a shepherd of a flock of nations. Let it not be imagined that the process of conversion from particularism to universalism is a morally elevated spectacle. The conqueror has to overcome many resistances in his own nature, survivals of his earlier training, habit, beliefs, and tastes. In purely personal terms, it is not without danger for a man to liberate himself from the virtues to which he was born, to rise about the venerable institutions of his ancestors, and to turn against his own comrades in arms. Without great strength of mind the process may lead to all kinds of foolish excesses or even to madness. The ruler is the first to feel the whole pressure of universal circumstance; the old ruling elements, less exposed to the new necessity, continue to be tied down by the old, necessarily particularist, virtues. A wise ruler would show outward respect to the conscript fathers, but he must know that they have ceased to be useful instruments of actual rule.

Universal rule, establishing itself, requires quick response to universal need and a ruthless pursuit of expediency. The ruler cannot use the scrupulous services of virtuous men. He must turn to personal favorites, irresponsible advisers, and hired experts dependent upon him alone. And such a class of civil servants he finds more readily in the anonymous mass of the slaves and the dispossessed than among the heirs of particularist aristocracies. His administration must, in order to survive, begin innocent of the ancient virtues and loyalties. In following his own star a universal ruler cannot afford to listen to his own pride, for "God permits no one to be proud except Himself."

Given a strong mind, adaptability, and a fine nose for self-interest, there is no reason why a conqueror should not transform himself into a universal ruler, a Caesar Augustus. There is nothing impossible, therefore, in the assumption that he should come to regulate transfer in universal rather than particularist terms. The universal state would in consequence acquire its own outer balance. But having reformed existing patterns of habit, the ruler would have disturbed the old balance (such as it was) between habit and myth. Before he can count himself safe, he has also to restore the inner balance of the universe.

During all the events which have gone before, the multitude, representing the lower kingdoms of cities, have moved in the appointed circle of toil and reproduction. The toiler—if not "slave by nature"—became at least slave to nature; differing in the unessential, the habit of multitudes was of one kind; hence, the corresponding systems of myth everywhere show a similar content, whatever forms they may have assumed. And as the natural priority granted to the function of reproduction forced the multitude to submission, vulgar myth would rationalize and fortify this priority. Gods of reproduction and fertility would take the seat of honor in the lower department of the divine hierarchy; a female dominance would dramatize the passive role assigned to the multitude. As the offering of transfer was their supreme duty in the outer kingdom, so did sacrifice constitute it in the inner. It is to be expected, therefore, that the base gods would have remained practically invulnerable to the dangers which cities passed through during the "times of trouble." Under the impact of peace and war multitudes would expand or contract in numbers, but their kind of habit would be little, if at all, affected. It is this underlying stability that permits the vulgar myths to enter the universal state filled with that vitality which comes from intact belief.

When cities grew, the ruling elements, representing the upper kingdoms in cities, had to pass through many sorts of change. While cities remained subject to objective necessities, there came to be more room for choice, and a kind of liberty, at the top. It was for this reason that social growth also meant a measure of social diversification. The ruling elements became the exponents of the individualization of cities; they were the true citizens and came indeed to compose the state. They created and maintained political institutions, churches, arts, literature, language, and most of what is generally understood as culture. The more cities grew, the more numerous, the more self-conscious, and the prouder did these elements become. But the same forces which created these elements made them predestined for self-conscious particularism. All that makes life worth living would seem to them to be embodied in particularist cultures; and as the human values had their birth and, so far, had grown only when incarnated in cities, they would have some reason to look with horror at one brutal—in its first manifestations—universal state. Each, in defending his own, would feel himself rising in defense of the human values themselves. It is natural, therefore, that in the "time of trouble" the citizens should fan particularism to a hysterical pitch; and the higher the vertical and cultural growth of participating cities, the better reason would they find to resist cultures which were different and inferior to their own. Reflecting the several needs and functions of the citizens, their gods would be more individualized, more changeable, and indeed more fickle than those of the multitudes. The process of social growth let the higher gods multiply and increase, arranging them in beautiful hierarchies. These have every reason to anticipate a "time of troubles" with dread. The impending change in habit will be dangerous in proportion to the previous vertical integration. The changes will drain away the belief upon which the gods depend. They must be expected to enter a universal state weakened; most of them angry, some puffed up, but all suffering from lack of nourishing belief.

These then are the mythical elements which the universal ruler inherits from the particularist cities, elements which he has to use in the great mutation now called for. On his left hand are the base gods: they are proletarian, by their undivided allegiance to necessity, universal in nature; they emerge after the "time of troubles" with undiminished vitality. On his right hand are the high gods: they are patrician, if not aristocratic, particularists in character, and weakened by loss of belief.

As the ruler above all stands in need of instruments inducing universal submission, his first, almost instinctive, impulse would be to turn to the left. The base and vital gods—in virtue of the historical necessity they serve—are universal in scope and have been used to promote blind obedience to authority among their worshipers. But while the attraction between the universal ruler and the proletarian gods is real, and perhaps irresistible, there is also between them a real conflict. And before casting his lot with them he must reconsider. The base gods, as we have seen, had their original habitat in a state of nature: if not prevented by higher gods, they will call man back with the authentic and original voice of obligation. They cannot help, therefore, being enemies to that vertical integration which first led to the need for a universal state and which continues to be necessary for its existence. The ruler, therefore, has good reason to fear these gods even when they bear gifts. His second impulse would be to turn to the high gods which had been also the gods of his fathers.

While the first impression of the low gods was attractive, the high gods show an angry and sulky mien. Threatened with being deprived of their lands, they are the natural enemies of universalism; accustomed to requiring some degree of virtue among their worshipers, they are not suited to serve as instruments of blind submission. But if they die, they will leave the old ruling elements—which were also society's technical agents—without inner support. These elements would inwardly be reabsorbed by the undifferentiated mass and lay down the burden of virtue. Hence, even the high gods serve a function essential to the ruler in supporting the vertical integration required for a universal state. Politically they are the born enemies of the ruler; technically and economically they are his necessary allies. It is not easy to see, therefore, how a surviving ruler can permit them to expire.

Tossed on the horns of this divine dilemma, there appear to be only two choices leading to survival. The first is to destroy the particularist gods of virtue in one fell stroke; but this is possible only if there can be found at once substitute technical agents to take up the economic function of the old ruling elements. In other words, the base gods have now to be habituated to virtue. The alternative is to keep the virtuous gods alive while gently educating them in universalism. This solution would leave the lower gods unchanged in the lower kingdoms. The first choice, while difficult, has not lacked learned and powerful friends.

Now, gods die a lingering death in a climate of disbelief; but vulnerable as they may appear they are not killed by frontal attack: the only way that has been found of disposing of them cleanly and swiftly is a physical liquidation of their worshipers. The first alternative, therefore, would involve the killing of all the old ruling elements. The ruler would dispose of the previous particularisms. Such a course is difficult but not impossible. It must be sudden and drastic and leave no time for the doomed elements to meet, conspire, or revolt. And instigating such a process, though on a partial scale, a universal ruler said: "It is not enough that you exterminate such as have appeared in arms. . . . The male sex of every age must be extirpated. . . . Let everyone die who has dropped an expression, who has entertained a thought against *me*. . . . Tear, kill and hew in pieces." [3] The techniques employed by the ancient ruler could, of course, be refined if the problem is to be approached in the objective spirit of applied science.

The liquidated elements represented the technical agents of society: they must now be replaced by new agents or the whole social structure will come tumbling down. The ruler must in each strategic position place men who are at once technically competent and submissive to universal rule. This task, while more delicate than the first, is not necessarily impossible. But it is necessary to warn against the notion that experience obtained in observing a partial process is applicable on the universal scale. Considering small, "primitive" universes the difficulties would indeed appear of minor magnitude. The low vertical integration implies that skills are few, relatively simple, and easy to acquire. Even the members of the ruling elements are fairly interchangeable and can at short notice be recruited afresh from the ranks. In a general way, therefore, the process seems most relevant to nations which have remained predominantly agricultural and in which more complex and more highly integrated habits of production have failed to take hold. But even more important, as long as we deal with a small universe, unification in it does not involve a break with the principle of particularism itself: while it is desirable to liquidate the ruling element in the conquered cities, the necessity does not as yet arise in the conquering city. For the universe transforms itself into a state which in turn, on the particularist basis, is placed in a greater universe. Hence, in

[3] Gibbon, *The Decline and Fall of the Roman Empire* (The Modern Library), vol. 1, p. 242.

particular, when a great city takes over a smaller one, it is not
difficult to replace the old ruling elements with persons recruited
in or by the conquering state. The nonglobal universe has the
further advantage of possible aid from abroad in form of exports,
and imports, of goods or capital. And as long as we deal with these
relatively early and simple phenomena of unification, there seems
little to object to in the ancient maxim: "Spare the lowly, and
pull down the proud." [4]

The circumstances which favored the liquidation process tend
to disappear, or lose importance, as we move into the global stage.
To reach this stage a very high previous integration both vertical
and horizontal is required. The technical agents needed to carry
out such integration have become numerous, their skills many and
complex, their tools delicate and expensive. The effective working
of the whole depends upon a nice adjustment between many interdependent parts. But theoretically another difference is more
important. Considering the previous process of unification, it is
now clear that it in reality represented steps from smaller to larger
particularisms. It is only now that it changes in quality for the
first time and becomes truly universal, in the sense of global. And
while previously the ruling element in the conquering state could
serve as an instrument, it now becomes necessary to liquidate that
element as well. We have reached a borderland between experience
and potentiality. And in order to understand the nature of the city
we must draw upon imagination and strain to visualize the waiting potentiality. We run up against the apparently fantastic; but
it should be remembered that the full significance of this excursion
can become apparent only at a later stage. We shall here draw some
of the broad outlines of the problem.

[4] Vergil, *Aeneid,* vi, 853.

The universal ruler—having to uproot particularism—would have to liquidate all the old ruling elements, including those in his native city. But if this boldness is not to lead to chaos, regression, and parcellation, he must already be in command of a party of followers trained in all the necessary skills and believing in the universal myths supporting them. Hence, *prior* to the final unification a potential universal ruler must have created, as it were, the upper kingdom of a universal state. We have conjured up a picture, not only of the "perfect" universal model but also a peculiar kingdom of shadows. Bringing it into power at just the right moment, the ruler would have achieved a perfect "response" to the "challenge" of universality. But while we need not doubt the elegance of the solution, we must, I suppose, inquire into the nature of the conditions under which it is possible of realization in the model which we know.

The universal ruler *in spe,* preparing his kingdom of shadows would, like all founders of states, be bound by the necessary and the possible. Hence, his first concern would be to construct a model universe transcending and anticipating experience. Whether or not the genius required for the task is forthcoming depends upon God. But supposing it does reveal itself, the next problem concerns the recruitment of followers who have to be kept together and trained to become full citizens of a kingdom that to most people will appear as little more than a mad dream.

The emerging city of shadows would have the professed ambition of liquidating and supplanting the ruling elements in all existing cities. This ambition, or so it would seem, makes it the enemy of all the upper kingdom; its recruiting-ground becomes the lower kingdom and the group of occasional "renegades" from the upper. The movement, therefore, can only become proletarian in origin and ethics. But it follows further that the world-conqueror —the victorious master of a particularist state, or combination of states—cannot be one and the same person as the master of the kingdom of shadows: a man cannot generally be expected to prepare the liquidation of himself and his necessary followers. It seems safe to conclude that the potential universal ruler, in this construction, is not a particularist ruler but a revolutionary. The potential universal kingdom becomes at once proletarian and revolutionary. It could on the whole expect neither sympathy nor support from any ruling element.

But turning our eyes to the lower kingdom—the natural habitat of this new movement—the conditions do not seem encouraging. The followers would need to be nourished and protected during periods of training and indoctrination. They would require leisure and some freedom from toil. In other words, like all ruling elements they become dependent upon transfer; it could in their case be forthcoming only as voluntary gifts from a sympathetic multitude. But even supposing the will be there, the hope for such gifts is almost nil as long as the rulers exact transfer up to (and *a fortiore* beyond) the optimum point, and as long as the multitude continues to give priority to the reproductive function and to be faithful worshipers of *Magna Mater*. We noted that her sway— even during the "time of troubles"—was not seriously threatened. Hence, as long as the dominion of the base gods in the lower kingdoms has not been undermined, so long can a potential universal ruler find neither friendship, support, nor gifts needed for his purpose. In spite of his proletarian affinities he finds, aspiring to rule, that he, no more than an actual ruler, can depend only upon the base gods of necessity. He requires the aid of a new god, conscious of virtue.

We were willing to go far beyond experience in order to find the potentiality contained in our model. But stretching our imagination to the utmost, we face, so far, the necessity of discarding the first alternative of universal unification. The man whom Fortune will call to become the "father of the coming age," must attempt the second alternative, must turn to the high particularist gods. From the height of his own necessity he will perceive that "everything that exists is the seed of that which shall come out of it." [5] But it remains to be seen if out of the seed of particularism there shall issue universalism.

[5] Marcus Aurelius, *To Himself*, IV, 36.

I I

The Death of the Gods

OF THE CITY

FOR, THE GODS OF EVERY CITY AND COUNTRY BEING MANY AND VARIOUS, AND THE ONE DESTROYING THE OTHER, THE WHOLE OF THEM IS DESTROYED BY ALL.—*St. Athanasius* [1]

THE RULER, WE CONCLUDED, WAS FORCED TO TURN to the higher gods; they should be persuaded to help create universal virtue, required for vertical integration. The disturbance in habit has called forth disbelief which, with some time-lag, would have manifested itself as increased pressure on the function of order; there would above all have been released a bitter struggle among the ruling elements for the fruits of rule: "power, riches, and the love of women." The first danger signals reach the ruler from the higher inner kingdom; there are omens and miracles, "presages from entrails, soothsaying, and prophecies." Oracles warn him that mankind has reached a crossroad leading either to "an ordered universe, or else a welter of confusion." The world, as stirring in a dream, expects the sudden light of a great mutation. But the ruler, aware of all this, has to proceed according to the narrow rules of his part.

Although "the gods, too, may be turned from their purpose . . .

[1] *Contra Gentes*, p. 24.

by libations and the odor of fat," they are not imposed upon by
bold and impious expediency. Antiquarian tellers of tales, be-
holding only the divine remains, may believe, with impunity, that
the gods were creatures of superstition and fancy. But the universal ruler, confronted with living gods, meets entities which
have all kinds of powers and functions. As wires charged with
high-voltage electricity can be manipulated only under the protection of formalized rites, so can the living gods be approached only
under the protection of pious ceremony. Rulers entering into the
inner kingdoms have done so in the seemly robes of *pontifex
maximus.*

We are told that when the cities were founded, gods, or sons of
God, acted upon the stage. They became the ancestors of rulers,
and were worshiped among the gods of the city. We witness now
—in the bright light of a universal stage—how the necessity that
let gods be born in the dawn of history calls forth also a universal
god. For great as the powers of chief priests may be, they are
not sufficient to meet the ruler's need. Priests and rulers are still
human: they may tell the people how to serve existing gods; but
they cannot order gods about, nor create new ones. Such acts belong to God. It is for this reason that the universal ruler must
claim divine attributes. Necessity forces him to scale heights of
vertiginous loneliness. It is doubtful whether or not man can
support such a burden; but if the ruler fails to live up to the
divinity thrust upon him, mankind has to pay the price. Let us
have faith, therefore, and imagine that the universal state is fortunate enough to find rulers who are humble enough to support
the burden of divinity and strong enough to rule themselves.

We are in the fortunate situation of having reports from such a
man. A universal ruler who was also a philosopher observed the

world from the pinnacle of lonely power and produced a unique record. Beyond the shifting fates of cities he found an underlying unity. "Constantly picture," he asks us, "the universe as one living organism . . . and note how all things are returned to a universal consciousness." [2] All parts hang together and "the mind of the universe is social." [3] Forced to rule, he becomes aware of the inner contradiction in addressing, as it were, a natural process in terms of outer might. He looks beyond contemporary experience in his search for a binding force in harmony with the social mind. He reaches insights which have the ring of authentic genius. "No one tires of service rendered," for "service is action after nature's way. Do not tire then of service gained by service given." [4] He is on his way out of the city of reason and clings to a vision of a universe governed not by fear but by obedience to some inherent force of attraction. This would involve nothing less than a new kind of social order.

But even this "heroic and divine kind of nature," harassed by present necessities and compelled by a feeling of urgency, turns back to the city. "While the hour yet tarries, what help is there? what but to reverence and bless the gods, to do good to man, 'to endure and to refrain'?" [5] Torn between the new vision and the old cares of rule, he asks us to "reverence and bless the gods." The gods he has in mind are not those of the vision; they are far from being either loving or universal, for they are the angry and particularist deities of the old cities. Invoking their aid, how can he turn them to his own purpose?

In each city there is a Palladium in which its deity is housed; it is sanctified by rite and ceremony and "adored as the preserver

---

[2] Marcus Aurelius, *To Himself,* IV, 40.   [3] *Ibid.,* V, 30.
[4] *Ibid.,* VII, 74.   [5] *Ibid.,* V, 33.

of the country and citizens." When a city is conquered by another, the victor cannot be safe before he has also conquered and subjugated the deity:

> The nation that I hate in peace sails by
> With Troy and Troy's fall'n gods to Italy.[6]

No city is safer than its Palladium. The universal ruler is, for the same reason as any founder of state, compelled to fashion a universal Palladium; but he cannot create his gods afresh; he needs the old ones to prevent a threatening regression. He erects a marble shrine, a Pantheon, worthy of the universal city and the divine company. To this house of many mansions he invites all the gods; they may come of their free will, but whatever the form of the invitation, it cannot very well be refused. Like contestants after a war the gods are asked to sit down together and by reasonable compromise create international peace. Meanwhile, the Pantheon serves as a kind of prison: the assembled gods cannot escape and stir up trouble in the outside world. And the ruler being a god —even if the most powerful—has to share the confinement of his guests.

The gates of the Pantheon must open to all the gods. The divine company, therefore, becomes strangely assorted: there are the high gods of noble cities; there are the base gods of the multitudes; there are the dissolute or impish deities of strange tribes. The return to absolute rule in the outer kingdom leads now to a kind of promiscuity in the inner kingdom. All the members of the Pantheon partake of divinity and are necessary for the whole. It becomes imperative to maintain the sovereign fiction of equality among them. To men who are not philosophers, one god will appear as good as

[6] *Aeneid,* 1, 67–68.

another; the choice between them, therefore, will be to many a matter of taste, if not indifference. The more closed the outer system becomes, the more open the inner. Gods of heroes share table and bed with *Cloacina,* goddess of the gutters. Poets and keepers of myth celebrate this new inner liberty, or anarchy of values, in plays and spectacles which tend to debase both what is divine and what is human. Many impute to the example of the gods the growing depravity of men. "For from Zeus they have learned corruption of youth and adultery, from Aphrodite fornication, from Rhea licentiousness, from Ares murders, and from other gods other like things, which the laws punish and from which every sober man turns away." [7]

It is thus easier to assemble the gods than to teach them how to thrive and how to agree: they know themselves too well to feel confidence in each other. Consider first the high gods which gave us most concern and which were now to become universalists. It is true that they were instruments of vertical integration; but it is true also that they derived their nourishment from local dominions: deprived of them it is difficult to see how they can survive. But gods are organized also on functional lines. In breaking the particularist habits of the gods the ruler deprives them of their old lands, and tries to organize a kind of hierarchy on purely functional (or horizontal) lines—breaking through the old vertical compartments. It would seem likely that the gods would resist this reform; but human-like they seem rather to become involved in jurisdictional disputes over the new competencies. The local gods served similar, but not identical, functions. In the crowded Pantheon (with its onrush of old and ever newly created deities) kindred gods may, so to speak, swallow each other up. This leads

[7] St. Athanasius, *Contra Gentes,* p. 26.

to an apparent swelling of some gods, and tends to keep down the divine population; but however puffed up some of them become, they do not increase in vigor. The confusion of the worshiper before the shifting divine spectacle weakens all the gods. This fusion and confusion of gods is so much the more dangerous as the vacuum created by their internal feuds tends to be filled, not by nothing, but by baser gods.

When the proletarian gods moved into the Pantheon they were of an expansive and lusty frame of mind. The ties which had kept them in bondage to higher gods had become unloosened and they had gained in divine status. They have in particular profited from the disappearance of foreign enemies and from the consequent disappearance of the harsh virtues imposed by local war gods. While the base gods used to masquerade in many local costumes, they were essentially of one kind—serving to guard the priority of the reproductive function. Hence, they, rather than the high gods, are suited for divine atonement. They now tend to unite into one great libidinous goddess—call her what you like: Astarte, the Great Mother, or *Libido*. Released from virtuous inhibitions she moves triumphantly from the outlying tyrannies into the Pantheon of the universe. Her services reach a new fervor in the multitude, influenced by spectacles, circuses, and mysteries.

But the rejuvenated goddess begins to cast her spells beyond her native domains in the lower kingdom. The greater tolerance in the inner kingdom, which lets one value appear as the equal of all other values, and the uncertain position of all the old ruling elements render the base gods socially acceptable. The previously virtuous, with the fringes of the dispossessed, welcome the occasion of laying down the burden of obligation and distinction, and the fall of their proper gods. Many satisfy a dark, anonymous craving in the soul by profaning the old altars, and heaping blasphemies on their suffering gods. *Libido* becomes a liberator and a guide back to the bosom of nature; men have forgotten her true face, so long hidden by the protective veil of habit and belief, and understand romantically her categorical imperative, that late nostalgia for the womb. But to men who are losing control over the present, the goddess offers the satisfaction of a feeling of superiority over a superstitious past. Like skiers swiftly descending a steep slope, they pity the slow effort of skiers still mounting. Many things conspire to the glory of the goddess; even the philosophic ruler cannot offend her, for she is necessary to promote universal submission. She thus moves forward in a moral vacuum partly created by herself.

For the quarrel between gods does not, as many believe, leave the city without gods. On the contrary, in a process of disintegration the gods are multiplied and men finally fall, by some law of social gravity, under the dominion of the lasting, sometimes tamed but never dead, gods of primordial nature. In this great movement of inner return it is not worship that disappears, but virtuous worship and life. And it is for this reason that "the gods by whom this empire stands [leave] all the temples and the altars bare." [8]

The Pantheon is a device of inner toleration; in the consumption of accumulated moral values it purchases for the universe a period of peace; it is useful in the removal of ancient particularisms, supplanting them with universal conflict of interest on the vertical line. But in devitalizing the gods of virtue it leaves the field more and more open to the base gods, universal only because of a common absence of virtue. Hence, we are, in fact, approaching that position in the inner kingdom which would have been

[8] *Aeneid,* II, 351–352.

realized if the ruler had at once liquidated the old elements. The method is slower and less bloody, and though it has given us a period of grace, we are faced with the same problem in the end.

The rulers are for necessary reasons already committed to the support of the old deities. The same reasons continue to prevent them from creating new gods. The best that rulers can hope for then is to try to prolong the existing state indefinitely. And if the universe is spared misfortunes—the greatest and the most likely being the accession to power of foolish or mad rulers—the agony of the high gods can be very long protracted. Habit, once established, carries a long way. Even after the ruling elements have become victims of enlightenment and have ceased really to believe in their proper gods and destiny, they may carry on much as usual —guided by obligation, ancient honor, and good breeding. A skeptical age is not opposed to ceremony; it is both cynically amused and emotionally attracted by paying its respects to the ever more corpselike images in the Pantheon. Indeed, this is the right climate for a late Golden Age; the pageantry of man and cities is never more splendid or opulent; the urbane and tolerant patricians become patrons of art and literature; cities rise in a new magnificence of marble; rulers and patricians alike give vent to a common desire for erecting public buildings and memorials; money is poured out to satisfy the jaded appetites of the rich, and in bread and circuses for the poor. Indeed, as the inner ties of society weaken, and the discipline of wars is no more, rulers find in the subventing of the sensual aspect of life a means of diverting social energies from politically dangerous activities.

And even if the spiritual climate becomes such that it is impossible to find any more rational and virtuous rulers, the social fabric is tough. After periods of misrule there may be energy left for repeated "rallies." Sparks from the old altars may be fanned into flame, and restore the semblance of virtue. But after each crisis that upsets the precarious equilibrium, recovery becomes slower and more incomplete; the social structure more brittle. Yet the gradual draining away of life may be so slow and so gradual as to be withdrawn from common observation. Man may take the universal state to be a permanent gift of nature, as lasting as it is outwardly majestic and awe-inspiring.

But *Caesar Divus* nears the journey's end. When the state is healthy, myths and gods represent social functions and are kept in balance by a hierarchy, being the supreme manifestation of social reason. The impulses of passion and the promptings of self-interest are kept in check by justice, supported by virtue. In a dying state myth and gods—beneath that smooth parliamentary decorum of the Pantheon—escape from their high tutelage. While formally subject to the divine ruler, they fall more and more under the dominance of the god of necessity. External pressures lead always to more specialization and departmentalization. Real or alleged principles and values have a right of representation in the inner kingdom. Powerful groups present their own gods and ideals, each clamoring for recognition. The synthetic deities of the demagogues, the thiefs, the experts, the merchants, the civil servants, and the harlots are symptoms of conflict and cannot resolve it. The divine ruler, whatever one may like to pretend, does not govern these interests; at the best he becomes an arbiter. Lacking a unifying principle, official religion becomes more and more utilitarian. It ceases to be concerned with long-time survival, and becomes an instrument in the ever-shifting power game within the state. Officials serving in the temples may sacrifice hecatombs to their principles; but they cannot compel devotion. They can systematize, organize, instruct, reform, and provide worshipers with informative booklets setting forth approved beliefs, and how each god should be worshiped and served. But even a loyal subject is unable to pay his respects to all the deities or pass a single day without offending some god or breaking some regulation.

With the evaporation of high belief the pressure of obligation becomes more and more insupportable. There arises a feeling of despair and futility. Because they lack a common purpose, individuals suffer from numberless inner conflicts and withdraw in droves from a society that fails to satisfy their inner needs. Many go in pursuit of private pleasure, power, and riches; a few seek in contemplation and renunciation of the world a lasting peace. In this world of multiplying frustration, the universal monsters have their birth.

It is a common error that a vertically constructed state can be destroyed by tidal upheavals from below. It is true, of course, that mob violence becomes part of all great disintegration processes; but the original cause releasing the train of events is to be sought within the ruling element itself. A wise ruler will worry little about the multitude so long as the Great Mother is securely enthroned; but he will distrust those most who are closest to him. With the disappearance of high belief and virtue, he must ever more depend upon cunning and outer might, and the fears they inspire, to safeguard his powers and his sacred person. And the more moral authority leaves the social body, the more awe-inspiring must the symbols and talismans of order become. Greater and greater is the trust that the ruler must put in the legions. To start with, the eagles seem to give safety. The virtues of loyalty and obedience have been tested in the long wars of conquest; but as the discipline of foreign wars ceases, and as the citizens who used to compose the legions withdraw from social service, the military change their character. They become less principled, more appetitive, and also aware of their own powers. To be kept in good temper the praetorian guards demand privileges and donations. And even while they may long maintain all the outward forms of veneration, they now know that the ruler, and in his person the universe, is at their mercy.

There is no timetable for these events; much depends on circumstance and chance. But once the guards have tasted their full powers, they will not easily be contained. United under good leaders they can exact any tribute they see fit, and even do what they will with the throne itself. Habit and self-interest would impose moderation; but the elements in question are what they are because of a lack in virtue. It seems fated, therefore, that in time they will become divided among themselves in the pursuit of selfish and partisan interests. This may perhaps at first sight seem an advantage to the ruler; but while dangerous when united, they are mortally so when divided. They represent the final power in the universe; their division means civil war. The contending factions, and the interests with which they are allied, will not any longer be satisfied with sucking the blood of the universe in peaceful transfer; they will begin to devour the body itself as they destroy cities and provinces, emptying them of men and gods.

In the final analysis, therefore, the disappearance of high belief and virtue leaves the city at the mercy of might. In a cumulative process the wielders of power impose ever more transfer until the universal balance becomes more and more out of joint. This leads to the dissolution of the skilled groups, to consumption of capital, to decreased productivity and surplus, and thus possible transfer. This starts a process of social contraction, both vertical and horizontal; at a point, the transfer required to keep the universe together will not be available, starting a nonreversible process of parcellation.

Interregnum has now descended on the universal scale. In character, effects, and frightfulness, it is far different from the local interregna that have gone before. Like a tidal wave it submerges the whole civilization. The panic, and the almost physical quality of the fear that envelops the world, is incapable of description. Nor is there any way of predicting what will be left when the wave recedes; how far destruction and parcellation will have proceeded, and how close to nature a succeeding civilization may have to start.

And with even more reason than the universal ruler we may conclude: "Again the same! That life too is dead. So likewise scan the many registers of ages and of nations; see how hard they strove, how fast they fell, and were resolved into the elements." [9]

[9] Marcus Aurelius, *To Himself,* IV, 32.

12

The Judgment

OF THE CITY

ALL THINGS FADE, AS A TALE THAT IS TOLD, AND
SOON ARE BURIED IN COMPLETE OBLIVION.

—*Marcus Aurelius* [1]

SOCIAL THEORY SHARES THE DANGERS and limitations common to all theory: it aims at constructing a system which is at once simple, logically consistent, and uncontradicted by experience. But reason is subject to error and experience itself is elusive. And there are dangers peculiar to the craft; while the social theorist strives to take the position of an observer, he remains in society and cannot without risking moral and intellectual disintegration, completely detach himself from it. Observation affects natural events, but this effect seems negligible when compared with the effect on social events: theory becomes itself a powerful force in social developments. Hence, united with innumerable visible and invisible ties to the phenomena, which he tries to describe and to understand, it would be a wonder if the social theorist were ever truly free from bias. He is not able to forget the terrible warning: "My brethren, by the bowels of Christ I beseech you, bethink you that you may be mistaken." [2] Having arrived at what

---

[1] Marcus Aurelius, *To Himself,* IV, 33.
[2] Oliver Cromwell (quoted by A. N. Whitehead, *Science and the Modern World,* Cambridge, 1938, p. 21).

appears to be the end of an inevitable social cycle, it is fitting then, that he should again question his judgments.

A model city may be more or less relevant to reality: it cannot pretend to cover the whole of experience, and still less the potentiality of experience. Our model was constructed with the purpose of laying bare the minimum conditions of social survival, but nothing prevents the real conditions from being more complex. On the other hand, new inventions and unforeseen occurrences may upset sequences theoretically expected, and solve problems unsolvable in the original terms. Social prediction is possible in a closed system only, and society remains, at least potentially, an open one. Considering the long march of events a social theorist is not justified in adopting determinism; he will point to certain alternatives and attempt to weigh probabilities of different order. And modest as the pretensions of social theory may be, they go, in fact, beyond those of history: for historical data are too few, too haphazardly collected, and too unreliable to lend themselves to statistical manipulation or prediction in respect to units as large and as ill-defined as "civilizations." Social theory has certain means of dealing with social process in general; but it has no more business than any other science to claim to know how a concrete situation will develop or to map out future events. Nor, of course, is it competent to entertain ideas as to the ultimate survival of man as a species.

The varied nature of social phenomena compelled social theory to proceed on a high level of abstraction. Society was conceived in terms of sequences and relationships of events, and could avoid defining either man or the natural universe per se. It was possible to avoid assumptions borrowed from either science or metaphysics. But theory observed that man stands in lasting relationships to environment, relationships which give rise to the social functions. The primary functions are production, reproduction, defense, and order; and as society develops there are added secondary functions determinate in terms of each successive level of vertical integration. And because the social resources and energies needed to satisfy these functions are limited (though not given once and for all) a city requires balance between the functions. The social balance (defining the outer survival conditions) must be conceived as an equilibrium moving through time. Neither man, nor his environment, is withdrawn from change; the equilibrium, therefore, must be conceived as dynamic; i.e., no matter how long it progresses each variable function, composing it, must remain bounded in values so as to protect the identity of the pattern.

The observation of any such pattern justifies the further assumption of a force in human nature that supplies the energy necessary for social events. If this necessary energy—call it instinct, passion, appetite, emotion, drive, urge, id, etc.—materialized spontaneously in a pattern of events compatible with social balance, the only danger to society would come from without. But observation of events shows patterns which can be meaningfully interpreted only by means of postulating a second force in human nature—parallel to instinct—called reason and defined as the force which renders man conscious of himself as an entity striving for agreement between ends (implicit in instinct) and means. Social reasons concerned with the requirements of social survival collides with private reason concerned with private ends. To secure social survival, private aims have to be subordinated to social ones. Might of rulers may bend habit and cause submission to the social will. But the instrumentality of force is of limited usefulness. Might uses up social resources and cannot be limitlessly expanded without upsetting the social balance. The subject responds to the suppression of his own ends with frustration creative of fears and hates which combine into monsters: to maintain balance, therefore, it is necessary to confine the monsters and limit the resources devoted to the function of order.

Surviving societies have, in addition to an outer kingdom of habit, developed an inner kingdom of myth. Myths reconcile men to particular habits, and to habit as a whole. For myths are fictions (the metaphysical or scientific truth of which is a matter of indifference), which if accepted as fact render it rational for a subject to submit to the social will. The form of myth changes, but its content is determinate in terms of each particular system of habit. If myths are believed they become, so to speak, invisible, appearing to the subject as one with "reality." Agreement between habit and myth constitutes inner social balance; if it is perfect the function of order is, in terms of force, reduced to zero. The interrelation of the two systems of habit and myth, of the Outer Kingdom and the Inner Kingdom composing society, gives rise to the characteristic social phenomena.

Habit tends to retain a degree of plasticity, but myth—masquerading as fact—becomes apparently as changeless as other established facts. The brittle nature of myth renders the system as a whole closed and apparently incapable of development. It is possible, with the aid of present assumptions, to explain why any social system—once it has come into being—can go on existing; but it is impossible to explain how societies can grow, change, or develop. Once the agreement between habit and myth is shaken, the destruction of myth would lead to overexpansion of the function of order with consequent social disintegration. In order to account also for the observed phenomena of social growth, or structural change, it is necessary to explain how one kind of social equilibrium can be changed into another kind.

The "initial state" of habit and myth, represented by the cities of Plato and Aristotle, happened to belong to a highly evolved society. Its habits could not be considered as original gifts of nature: they must be thought of as the result of a process of historical development. What appeared changeless must be conceived as the product of previous developments of cities themselves apparently as changeless as the Republic. The city, therefore, must have found in the past the means of breaking out of nature, and of protecting its successive, precarious equilibria from a return to it. Hence, in order to explain how the Republic, and all other vertically integrated cities, could have arisen, we inferred a further force, breaking existing equilibria, creating new ones, and called it genius.

Habit creates a feeling of obligation, being in its most elemental terms a categorical imperative saying "you must because you must." There is a feeling of obligation in respect to each habit, and all obligations join together into a totality of obligation supporting all habits. This totality of obligation—call it, if you like the "moral law within," or the moral conscience—tries to compel men to obey all habits which have happened to come into being. Similarly, myth which rationalizes habit becomes subject to belief. It supports individual myth, but combines into a totality of belief which supports all myth. From the viewpoint of the subject, perfect inner social balance is a state in which there is agreement between total obligation and belief, a state in which, therefore, the individual is perfectly adjusted to social environment.

In order to explain how the Republic could have arisen we must imagine genius to be a force powerful enough to "challenge" both obligation and belief, break old forms and create new equilibria on higher levels of integration. It is natural to imagine that genius, and the "challenge" it represents, is constantly present in society. But in order to be followed by a successful "response," i.e., social growth, certain conditions must be met. The difficulties of change rest mainly in the inner kingdom.

Social growth presupposes a process that can be compared with an inner mutation of society. Without repeating what has been said in detail, the mutation is a complex process through which myths are changed—without such change being perceived by the subjects—to fit a state of habit, potential in the "challenge" of genius. Social mutations are neither necessary nor automatic phenomena; we know them to be inseparable from the risk of disintegration or a return toward nature. But of originally innumerable "challenges" a few must have been thought of as leading to success; there must have arisen out of nature many small cities, some of which had the vitality, and the good fortune, to pass a series of successful mutations, rising vertically and expanding horizontally. During a long process of growth and differentiation, some of the seeds grow into larger entities. Successful cities combine into societies of cities, or political universes. By means of the defense-function the closed city systems come into contact. And if social growth is continuous, less successful cities will become absorbed by more successful ones, until a certain efficiency of habit must be thought as necessitating a universal state. War serves to reestablish social balance in growing cities. The process of social growth and the unification of cities into larger units proceeds under risk; the global state is present as a potentiality in the social process, but whether or not society will reach this end is an open question. Indeed, argument rather favors pessimism;

for the efficiency of habit needed for the realization of a global state is so high as to render wars more and more self-defeating, proceeding on ever higher levels of total risk. But great as the risk may be there is nothing impossible in the assumption that, finally, in one of the games of musical chairs played by civilizations, one city will be left in sole possession of the globe. The defense-function, previously unbounded, will be eliminated, and it becomes possible to concentrate on the inner risk.

When the city emerged out of nature, men were divided into two groups—the rich (the rulers) and the poor (the multitude). Growth implied further vertical integration; it implied increased surplus, transfer, and the addition of new secondary functions and special groups—administrators, educators, engineers, philosophers, and so on—nourished out of the surplus. The complexity of the social balance increased, and reached its maximum when habit had become so efficient as to make possible and necessitate a global state. The misuse of transfer was a danger born with the city itself. And this danger increased as the city grew. For the higher its integration, the greater becomes the social contraction when the secondary functions upon which it rests are starved. Therefore cities, having risen above nature, found it necessary to train the rulers in virtue, steeling them against arbitrary choice, and to habituate the multitude in submission. And the reasons which compelled particularist rulers to construct a dualistic city would compel a universal ruler to reconstruct it on the universal scale. But the difficulty of reconstructing order is proportionate to the previous degree of vertical integration. For the bearers of the secondary functions are, by necessity, particularist elements.

The first condition of perpetuating universal rule is to secure an outer social balance, and in order to do this the ruler needs tools submissive to universal rule. He recruits a class of experts, hirelings, and favorites to carry out what is politically expedient, while he leaves, if he is wise, the old ruling elements their non-political status. But in order to secure the new habit-system, the ruler should create universal myth and get it accepted. He must assume control over the inner kingdom and try, by administrative means, to force the great mutation from particularism to universalism.

The difficulty of universal value-formation is reflected in the institution of Pantheon. The mobility of habit—inseparable from social growth, a "time of troubles," and the creation of a universal state—is dangerous to high belief. The upper kingdoms become enlightened, ancient myths lose their meaning, particular beliefs, and then all beliefs, begin to evaporate. Obligation, while strong enough to support traditional modes of behavior for prolonged periods, becomes, at length, individually irrational, and begins to be felt as a frustrating burden. But the multitude, while during this period expanding or contracting in numbers, has not changed habit; and in the universal state the gods of submission combine and expand. Formed by common necessity, they become the ready tools of universal rule. While high belief evaporates, the vacuum is being filled by ascending low belief; the inner differentiation between rulers and multitude is being rubbed out; all men tend to become fused into one large, undifferentiated mass. This development deprives the universe of the virtuous restraint needed in its technical agents (threatening indirectly the efficiency of habit) but it releases certain political effects which overshadow these indirect ones.

In the absence of consent to rule, the ruler must depend upon might and the fear that it inspires. The state divides into contending factions, guided by self-interest, and transfer to the physical arm of order has to be speeded up. Power finally gravitates to the military. Surplus is fed to the legions or is wasted in internal strife. The longer this situation continues, the less become the resources left to satisfy the secondary functions and the capital formation required to maintain the efficiency of habit. After a point productivity will begin to decrease: greater relative transfer is required to produce a given absolute amount of transfer and so on in a cumulative and, finally, nonreversible process. The universe moves into the great interregnum when

> . . . every thing includes itself in power,
> Power into will, will into appetite;
> And appetite, a universal wolf,
> So doubly seconded with will and power,
> Must make perforce an universal prey,
> And last eat up himself.[3]

The interregnal dissolution does not appear incidental nor, in so far as we can see, due to avoidable mistakes. The process may be speeded up by foolish rulers, but it cannot be prevented by wise ones. In the process of its growth the city ran into the great, but not necessarily fatal, risk of war. This risk tended, to some extent, to overshadow the fact that since the founding of the city the rulers and the multitude had formed two cities which were, as Plato said, at war with each other. But when in the universal state external war was no more and military discipline relaxed, this internal warfare became fatal. In the end, the upper kingdom, incapable of maintaining its own "noble lie," sank back towards the state of nature against which it had revolted.

[3] Shakespeare, *Troilus and Cressida,* Act 1, Scene 3, lines 119–124.

It may be impossible for a ruler to educate the low gods in virtue. But the affinity between them and the universal state is obvious and it is not impossible, at least in theory, that genius may succeed where might failed. The growth of society led to the removal of the vertical partitions of nations. Universal survival now requires the removal of the horizontal partition of class. And contemplating the problem of universal virtue genius inquires into the nature of God, for in the concept of Him the fate of society is hidden. And having "learned that the greatest and supreme and the most comprehensive community is that which is composed of men and God, [it asks] . . . why should not . . . a man call himself a citizen of the world, why not a son of God?" [4] To a universal god, men are brethren and his worshipers members of one high kingdom. "Do you not know, that as a foot is no longer a foot if it is detached from the body, so you are no longer a man if you are separated from other men. For what is man? A part of a city, of that first which consists of gods and men; then of that which is called next to it, which is a small image of the universal city." [5] To create lasting order: men should "attach themselves to God. . . . Whatever God wills, a man should also will." It is urgent then to find the will of God, and now in the search for "divinity, the soul advances until, having risen above everything that is foreign to her, she alone with Him who is alone, beholds, in all His simplicity and purity, Him from whom all depends, to whom all aspires, from whom everything draws its existence, life and thought . . . [she] is overwhelmed by love; with ardor desiring to unite [herself] with Him, enhanced by ecstasy." [6] And henceforward "those who have admired

[4] Epictetus, *Discourses,* book I, chap. 9.　　[5] *Ibid.,* book II, chap. 5.
[6] Plotinus, *Complete Works* (K. S. Guthrie), I, p. 50–51.

His sovereign beauty . . . [thrill] in a painless orgiasm, [love] with a genuine emotion, with an ardor without equal, . . . [and disdain] those things which formerly they characterized as beautiful." [7]

If in the dying city, then, "there is one who says *Dear City of Cecrops!* wilt thou not say *Dear City of God?*" [8]

[7] *Loc. cit.*   [8] Marcus Aurelius, *To Himself,* IV, 23.

PART II
The City as Love

FOR LAW IS ORDER, AND GOOD LAW IS GOOD ORDER;
BUT A VERY GREAT MULTITUDE CANNOT BE
ORDERLY : TO INTRODUCE ORDER INTO THE UN-
LIMITED IS THE WORK OF DIVINE POWER—OF SUCH
POWER AS HOLDS TOGETHER THE UNIVERSE.

—Aristotle

I3

Founded on Faith

FOR WHAT OTHER END DO WE PROPOSE FOR OUR-
SELVES THAN TO ATTAIN TO THE KINGDOM OF
WHICH THERE IS NO END.—*St. Augustine* [1]

THE CITY OF REASON was a construct which aimed at clarifying
the conditions of enduring social life. Pursuing a single aim, it
became anchored in the main stream of our intellectual tradition.
It interpreted meaningfully many otherwise disconnected social
phenomena and theories; some of the relationships discovered
seemed of universal validity; and all could, if we chose, be supported by an impressive mass of illustration. The results are uncontradicted, it seems, by experience; but this is not to say that
they account for the whole of experience. Indeed, many phenomena which are typical of Western society, in particular, have
failed to find a place in the first model. Theory has the further
duty, then, of accounting for these phenomena, and it is to this
remaining area that the second book addresses itself.

We could go to the task variously. But for reasons which will
become clear as we proceed we use an indirect approach. In terms
of probable survival, the first model was little better than an
outright failure. In logic, therefore, it seems natural to seek the

[1] *City of God,* book XXII, chap. 30.

reasons for this failure, and to inquire whether or not it is possible to find an alternative route leading to social survival. And as in the first approach many social phenomena fell in order, so, we may hope, others will follow in this second approach.

In retrospect all phenomena of social disintegration seem traceable to the common root of change. The city was safe as long as it had achieved, and was able to maintain, harmony between the outer and inner kingdoms. But the city was placed in the flux of circumstance; and an overwhelming probability warns us that in the course of time disintegration of the social balances is bound to occur. Existing order is undermined by the workings of man's imagination, or by the force of genius. Survival comes to depend upon the city's capability of "responding" to recurring "challenges" with reintegration into ever higher equilibria. The risk of social disintegration is cumulative in a series of "challenges" and "responses."

Social change is primarily change in social habit: but continued balance requires corresponding change in the supporting system of myth which—masquerading as fact—appeared prima facie unchangeable. This view of the nature of myth has not been foreign to theory, but it is contradicted by experience: in social mutation we found periods in which myth was apparently plastic, adaptable to new habit, and thus capable of admitting social growth. And in order to investigate the concrete risk of social disintegration, it became necessary to inquire into the nature of the social mutation, a possible though not a necessary or inevitable phenomenon.

Again, in this inquiry let us distinguish between two kinds of projections in the inner kingdom: myth and norm. While closely interrelated, they are at each moment separate and distinct. Myths are fictions (the intrinsic "truth" of which is a matter of social indifference) rationalizing social habit in terms acceptable to private intellect. Norms are values, or notions of desirable action (which, as such, can be neither "true" nor "false") attached to some unrealized, or even unrealizable, future system of habit. They lack originally all anchorage in social experience. They reflect instinct and, therefore, run the danger of being carried away by subjective fancy, private interest, or partisan passion. Periods of social unrest bring forth abundant crops of conflicting norms; indeed they are inseparable from the process of social disintegration and represent, in one aspect, vehicles of interregnum. While apparently under the dominion of the subjective, and thus hostile to objective order, the norms are, under another aspect, seeds of social growth. Myths, which were not inherited from the state of nature must be thought of as having started their careers under the auspices of norm. Social growth, therefore, implies a process in which, out of an abundance of norms, some are captured, tamed, and made to serve the city. And arbitrary as norm may appear in general, myth-destined norm must, like myth, submit to social discipline. In other words, to permit reestablishment of social balance, there must be found a way of determining a priori what norm is capable of becoming myth; more generally, men must invent "an art of making gods." [2]

It is for this reason that norms, aspiring to myth-hood, had to be referred to a potential social system in which nascent norms, or ideals, were already visualized as myth supporting a new stable system of habit. The construction of such ideal cities of the future required high genius. And as actual cities became more evolved and more enlightened, it became more difficult to instill belief in

[2] ps. Apuleius, *Asclepius,* 37 (=Augustine, *City of God,* book VIII, chap. 24).

any system of myth once belief had been shaken. The outer might
of rulers may bend habit, but myth-supporting belief could not
be commandeered. A reformer could ill afford then to enlighten
people about the nature either of myth or of norm. He had to
protect existing myth in order to safeguard the integrity of belief
needed to stabilize a new habit system. He had to smuggle norm
into the system of myth, letting both masquerade as fact. The
reformer, therefore, is wont to speak in a parable; "that seeing
they may see, and not perceive; and hearing they may hear, and
not understand." [3] And social change in the first model tended to
take the total and sudden character of a mutation. Social growth
could be visualized under the figure of leaps from one equilibrium
to another: each leap involved risk, and a series of leaps cumulative
risk. Truly, a few cities have risen to "respond" to more than a
few "challenges"; and many have been left behind and are no
more. Successive and successful mutations, though always possible
in theory, become ever less probable in practice. Hence, it may
perhaps be said that the risk of social disintegration represents the
price paid for social growth. And in order to found lasting cities
ways of growth should be discovered less hazardous than those of
mutation. In other words: Can we conceive and construct a city,
not in terms of a series of separate and unstable equilibria, but
in terms of one changeable equilibrium permitting a continuous,
bounded process of growth?

Social change is no new concern. It was never far from the
thoughts of the founders of the city. Why, then, did they fail to
visualize society in terms of process, and why did they, at best,
achieve a kind of imitation of the dynamic? For the social mutation represents, in fact, growth achieved at the cost of revolution

[3] *St. Mark,* IV, 11–12.

and at the risk of chaos. If an answer to such questions is possible, it would lead us to, and beyond, the sacred groves of early metaphysics. But in a more narrow sense, we perceive in the model city that a static theory on the whole tends to fit the limited range of early vision and experience, an experience then further stabilized by the reaction upon it of theory itself. Moreover, static habits of thought tend to result from a primacy of reason over experience. Closing the book of experience, the construct of right reason, looking for lasting social life, becomes one, and it becomes changeless: the diversities of actual life will appear as shortcomings due to the imperfect realization of the rule of reason. Social change will appear possible only along one line, beginning, as Marx thought, in nature, and ending in the one perfect city. The integration and disintegration of cities will appear as an advance towards, or a retreat from, these two points.

In flashes of deep insight, Aristotle almost broke the fetters of static rationalism. He introduced the potential as an element of theory, and in the concept of perfect virtue, co-existing with the virtue of a good citizen of any existing city and relative to it, he came near to conceiving a continuous and gradual process of change. In the inner striving for perfect virtue there was an element which supplied the city with virtue appropriate to a future state and thus with inner stimuli to change. But pregnant with consequence as these concepts are, in the end they led back to the static; for the determination of perfect virtue remained the monopoly of resaon. To break through to the truly dynamic process it is necessary first to reexamine the postulates of theory.

The competency of reason, as here defined, is limited to means-end relationships. Under given assumptions—in a closed universe —the habits of thought created by the primacy of reason seem to fit experience. But in an open universe the situation changes. Indeed, the growth of systematic knowledge in the field of science presupposes a previous liberation of thought from the rational primates of ancient philosophy. Science granted priority to experience, made theory fit the observed data, and hunted down error by means of controlled experiment. But this change in the intellectual center of gravity was originally more revolutionary and less easy than it may appear to later generations. For leaving behind the preoccupations of static and rationalist thought, the continued work of reason came to depend, not upon reason itself, but upon the acceptance of a new basic assumption as to the nature of the universe. Man's growing control over physical environment began when, religiously inspired, he liberated himself from a priori postulates, or the concept of innate ideas, and turned directly to experience "content with simple faith in the order of nature."[4] In explaining the observed data and relationships reason increasingly submits to a primate of experience, and becomes, pragmatically speaking, capable of feats previously beyond its competence. But note that the triumph of reason, as exemplified in science, goes back to this leap of faith, originally neither rational nor simple; note also that current social theory—while freely borrowing nomenclature and specific techniques from the sciences— has drawn back before a corresponding leap of faith. Many theoretical systems think of themselves as dynamic and scientific; but they remain, on the whole, under the dominance of rational a priori postulate. It is under the spell of the ancients that the great contending systems of social thought now present themselves as independent and mutually exclusive conceptions; it is in con-

[4] A. N. Whitehead, *Science and the Modern World* (Cambridge, 1938), p. 65.

sequence of such a priori rationalism that no bridge leads from the one to the other and that the only arbiter between the contenders has become bare might. Now, the apparent need for new departures in social science implies neither the need nor the necessity of dispensing with static theory: change and rest are both conceptually necessary. Dynamic theory requires the starting point, or the platform, of a static theory. For "mere change without conservation is a passage from nothing to nothing. The final integration yields non-entity. Mere conservation without change cannot conserve. For, after all, there is a flux in circumstance, and the freshness of being evaporates under mere repetition." [5]

The reluctance of social theory to move forward is explained partly by the width of the chasm ahead. It was thought, at least to start with, that the natural universe was closed, offering a frame of reference for study and experiment that did not change. But dealing, not with a stable society, but with a society in a process of birth, growth, and decay, there is a necessary divorce between observation and experience. Relevant experience is present largely in the form of potentiality, and social experience itself is expansive and floating. Hence, speaking dynamically, what is required in social science is not only faith in a natural order of society, but also faith in a natural order of potential social growth. And however slow such a faith has been in permeating social theory, it is of ancient date and has long been an active force in the social process itself. For "so is the kingdom of God, as if a man should cast seed into the ground, and should sleep and rise night and day, and the seed should spring and grow up, he knoweth not how. For the earth bringeth forth fruit of herself; first the blade, then the ear; after that, the full corn of the ear." [6]

[5] *Ibid.*, p. 250.   [6] *St. Mark,* IV, 26–28.

We have here collected the intellectual elements which are needed for the construction of a new city. It would be possible to build it *ex novo*. But when we first raised the fundamental problems of social survival we found ourselves in company with the masters of Hellas. And considering the progressively more important role played by theory as an integral part of social experience, it seemed necessary to proceed in terms supplied by tradition itself. And when we again set out seeking a more lasting city, we fall into company with another master and can remain on the great highway of tradition. Only it should be understood that we are neither interested in, nor competent to explain, Christian thought as a whole; we select, as hitherto, such elements as are logically necessary in the construction of theory, elements which, if not historically given, would have had to be invented fresh for our purpose.

But before proceeding, remember that Jesus, unlike Plato, did not leave behind a systematic account of his thought. The Gospels contain reports of His life, miracles, and words; but His teachings have been sifted by many minds which—even if inspired by the "spirit of truth" [7]—are in no way equal to that of the kindler of the flame. The apostles had to select sayings and events: for "if they should be written every one, I suppose that even the world itself could not contain the books that should be written." [8] In moving on we are not free from awe; but we share few of the scruples of current theology. Jesus we know through the mirror of the Gospels. If these, and we doubt it, were the fruits of the creative imagination of persons unknown, the truths ascribed to Jesus would be no less. We are concerned with the logical con-

[7] *St. John*, xvi, 13.   [8] *Ibid.*, xxi, 25.

sistency and the theoretical necessity of His teachings, not with the ways by which they have been communicated to us.

But men, enlarging the horizon of experience, seem almost bound to meet difficulty of communication. Contemporary language does not suffice, and such language as is freshly created meets the resistance of established habits of thought. The innovator is likely to resort to symbols and parables, which have to create their own meaning and response. Indeed, they tend to become generally understandable only in terms of the new experience they create and the new questions that they raise. And the greater the forward leap of genius, the less are we able to understand what it tries to say. And the farther it takes us into the potential, the greater is the effort of imagination required. This effort we are bound to resist, but to the extent we succeed in this, we close the doors to an understanding of the process of growth, for it consists essentially, as we have already seen, "in supposing possible what is actually impossible in a given society, in imagining what would be its effect on the soul of society." [9] This effort must be repeated by each generation, which, in its turn, is compelled to leap into the actually impossible; and this is the reason why a dynamic morality must seem to "border upon paradox, and even contradiction." [10] This is also the reason "why the first morality [of myth] is comparatively easy to formulate, but not the second [of norm]. For our intelligence and our language deal in fact with things; they are less at home, representing transition and progress." [11]

Returning, then, to the main theme, and leaving behind ra-

---

[9] Bergson, *The Two Sources of Morality and Religion*, p. 69.
[10] *Ibid.*, p. 50.   [11] *Ibid.*, pp. 50–57.

tional postulate, we must rid ourselves of the last vestiges of the intellectual habit of formulating a priori social ends. This liberates us from the fruitless search after the *summum bonum* which, it is said, society ought to desire. It lies in the nature of the seed to grow: it contains, as in code-script, the answer to its own "purpose." A good gardener will try to find out and meet the conditions conducive to rich growth; he will observe and he will experiment; but he will not, lifting the seed in his hand, tell us how that seed ought to grow. A good theorist will be like that gardener. He will try to find out the conditions for a more abundant social life; but he will not, *ex cathedra,* prescribe how future society ought to evolve. The future of the city is dormant in it. By solving problems as they arise, we are forming the future, and creating also new problems to be solved in a never-ending process. The future is contained, and is capable of modification, in the present moment. And provided that we could find the laws of social growth in a pluralist universe, obedience to these laws would result in harmony and there would be no need to take "thought for the morrow: for the morrow shall take thought for the things of itself." [12]

The belief in a potential order inherent in society, liberates us from the search after a priori "ends." But it does not leave the field open for the lawless and the arbitrary. On the contrary, it renders observation of society, and obedience to its laws, more imperative. To find out these laws is the task of the social theorist. The knowledge of them is not innate; and obedience to them, if found, comes far from easy. If it were not so, men would long since have found the way leading to the felicity of abundant life.

[12] *St. Matthew,* VI, 34.

But "broad is the way that leadeth to destruction, and many there be which go in thereat. . . . Narrow is the way, which leadeth unto life: and few there be that find it." [13]

Danger of social growth was encountered chiefly in the inner kingdom. Myth and belief were anchored in the past. And when now, in a study of growth, we turn towards the future, we turn also from myth to norm, which reflects what is to come. In the Aristotelian construction, where we first met with norm, it was still subject to reason. It was made operative through legislators, and it did not dare to show its face openly. It took part in the masquerade of myth. But having discarded rational postulate, it is time for norm to unmask itself. Norms, considered in themselves, are parts of a social process. But as norm tries constantly to form new habit, it tends to render itself superfluous in a continuous process of new development. To the extent habit is to change, norm, though in each instant necessary and determinable, becomes subject to birth, growth, and decay. This conscious mortality of norm forces it to discard the pretense of being factual. Norms considered in isolation are neither reasonable nor unreasonable; they are meaningful only in the light of a social process conceived as a whole. Constant belief in either particular habit or particular norm becomes then a frictional element in development and has, in a pure dynamic process, to be discarded. These relationships, though in the logical sense simple, meet with a certain resistance in terms of still-prevailing habits of thought, and a certain slow carefulness is perhaps needed when we turn to them.

Consider, then, that the totality of belief was made up of a sum

[13] *Ibid.,* VII, 13, 14.

of particular beliefs fitted to particular habits, and that interlocking obligation and belief tended to stabilize the system as a whole.
Any change tended to weaken each part of the system, but most
seriously totality of belief. Devotion to unchangeable norm would
lead, therefore, in a process of growth, to a constant destruction
of particular beliefs and so prevent a totality of belief from ma-
terializing. Hence, if we are to have a development of norm without provoking an interregnum, it is necessary to transfer belief
from norm in particular to the process of norm-formation. Faith
in a particular norm must result not from the alleged rationality
of it but from faith in the process as a whole out of which it comes.
Faith, therefore, having its focus in potentiality, is capable of sus-
taining disagreement between actual habit and norm. Faith is as
elastic as belief is brittle; it expects the tension between the real
and the ideal; it is invulnerable to the impact of outer events.

It is easy to perceive, therefore, how the emphasis on the dynamic leads from myth to norm, from particular beliefs to a
totality of faith. While myth is the shadow of reason, norm expresses the emotional, value-forming part of man. And as the
projection point moves from the past to the future, the primacy
moves from the outer kingdom to the inner kingdom. In the old
construct belief was determinate only in terms of preëxisting
norm. The movements in the inner kingdom come to determine
not only the construction of the outer, but also the rate of change
of the construction as a whole. And to the extent that people have
faith in the natural order of norms, the inner balance of society
is safe. The process of change assumes a gradualness foreign to
the mutation, and there is no occasion for interregnal interrup-
tions. In the dynamic construct the apparent paradox—"seek ye
first the kingdom of God, and his righteousness; and all these

things shall be added unto you." [14]—dissolves itself into logical necessity.

But this new departure in the inner kingdom rests on the faith that there exists, a natural order of norm that can be discovered and implemented. If the new city is to be more than a dream, we need to learn about norm-formation. Not without reason did the ancients fear the lawless nation of norm, to them indistinguishable from the anarchy of appetite and will. We are moving in a world, not only of growth, but of "dangerous conflict."

[14] *Ibid.,* VI, 33.

14

A CITY

Governed by Love

THE WONDER OF WONDERS IS THAT MAN COULD FIND
THE DIVINE NATURE AND GIVE IT EFFECT.

—*ps. Apuleius* [1]

WE HAVE ASKED whether or not it is possible to construct a model
of a process of social change to take the place of mutation. In the
first approach it was found that this attempt forced us to give
up the priority of reason, and to assume that there existed in the
social universe a potential order discoverable by man. It forced
us to discard the construct of myth—the child of reason—and to
depend upon the construct of norm—the child of desire. It is now
necessary to examine the conditions under which a normative
development of society is thinkable.

Norm is no newcomer to our thought; but it remains in many
respects a stranger. Further acquaintance with it leads us to reconsider that vital area of social growth where man invented the
"art of making gods." Norm, we found, was an expression of
man's primary energies, inseparable from the flow of events con-
stituting society. But so far, socially operative projections of norm
had to accept the discipline of social reason and had to be forced
into the general category of myth: norms were always, in some

[1] *Asclepius,* 37.

way, referred to a primary system of actual or potential habit. But having left behind the primacy of reason as lawgiver, we have to come into immediate contact with that force which prompts men to desire and to desire to act.

This primary force can originally be considered neither rational nor irrational, neither good nor evil. For the criteria of rational and moral judgments can be supplied only by existing cities, or by cities conceived as existing. The ancients, therefore, were wise in their generation when they assigned moral innocence to man in a state of nature, and let the birth of the city be mixed up with the first knowledge of good and evil. But in existing cities it is not easy to maintain this view of human nature considered in itself. Men have to accept habits imposed upon them and only exceptionally do they embrace habits spontaneously and joyfully. Indeed, they generally submit to socially needful habit only if intimidated by fear or deceived by myth. Frustration of the many impulses of instinct involved the city in "dangerous conflict" and led to the birth of the monsters. It is natural, therefore, that an observer, placed in the city, would see "human nature" only as it has been long molded in social forms and inflamed by unceasing social pressures. Noting the same phenomena, generation upon generation, he would conclude that human character observed in the city is, in fact, identical with human nature itself. "Measuring themselves, and comparing themselves among themselves," [2] they could not know themselves. It seems inevitable, therefore, that from such a place an observer would conceive human nature as corrupt and naturally sinful. He would seem predestined for social pessimism and predestined to be the victim of the short-sighted Manichaean heresy. And when we set out, beyond the old

[2] 2 *Corinthians*, x, 12.

city, in search of new order, it would be perilous to listen to the voices of people left behind. We must approach human nature with eyes innocent of the necessary illusions and prejudices of the old world.

The founders of the old city were not altogether unaware that there existed some means of dealing with man's impulses other than those of a priori reason. Aristotle talks about a divine power that without compulsion "holds together the universe"; the Stoics go even further, consciously looking for a world-city governed by some universal power of attraction. Plato himself points to a "necessity not geometrical, but another sort of necessity which lovers know, and which is far more convincing and constraining to the mass of mankind." [3] Still, so far we have not seen our way to liberating this underlying power and to using it directly for social purposes without at the same time releasing a process of disintegration. But it is precisely toward the lawless nation of norm, desire, and appetite that the founders of the new city turn like conquerors.

This great forward movement, impossible in the terms of previous experience, presupposes a new element. The Stoics had pushed a number of concepts beyond the limits of the old order: they "proclaimed themselves citizens of the world, and added that all men were brothers, having come from the same God. If they did not succeed in drawing humanity after them, it is because Stoicism is essentially a philosophy," [4] speaking the language of reason rather than the language of emotion to which they, in the last instance, should have appealed. They remained rationalists in essence, distrusting human nature, and many ended, therefore, in a pessimism so radical that suicide appeared as a good. And even

[3] *Republic,* 458d.   [4] Bergson, *The Two Sources,* p. 52.

Plotinus, in the authentic ecstacy of contemplation, remained predominantly in reason. But a normative order among the emotions, if at all possible, must be thought "the outcome of an emotion, unique in its kind, which [at first] seemed to baffle expression, and yet had to express itself . . . the emotion which precedes the image, which virtually contains it, and is to a certain extent its cause." [5] If a new advance is to be thinkable, it is for such a new emotional element that we have to look. Theory deduces from certain phenomena the presence of a certain force; while unable to follow this force beyond a certain stage, theory must count it a datum. Historical observation tells us that with Christianity a new force entered into the social universe. There is a definite change in the spiritual climate which cannot avoid being reflected in any faithful reporting; and we find movements inexplicable in the terms of previous experience alone. In the physical universe we used to account for the behavior of given entities by imagining them to be in the grip of certain forces. This method holds good in the social universe, and social theory has to rest primarily on the observed behavior of cities; but on the other hand it would reflect a certain obscurantism if we should refuse to recognize that men in the grip of social force, deducible from their behavior, have the capability of reporting their reactions to this force. While it would be dangerous (though perhaps not impossible) to base theory on such subjective reports, and while the inner experience in the strictest logical sequence falls outside our subject, it is still prudent to take it into account. The fuller inner experience of Christianity may be rare and strike many as a tale carried back by travelers from strange lands; but it forms part of social experience in a larger sense.

[5] *Ibid.*, p. 39.

In the circumstances we can do no better than to recall what witnesses have said. The first part of the Christian experience is described by the mystics in words almost identical to those used by Plotinus. The soul about to be swept forward "does not directly perceive the force that moves it, but it feels an indefinable presence, or divines it through a symbolic vision. Then comes a boundless joy, an all-absorbing ecstacy or an enthralling rapture: God is there, and the soul is in God." [6] But what distinguishes the Christian experience is a subsequent movement of return to do God's work. "There is an irresistible impulse which hurls [the true mystic] into vast enterprises" [7] foreign to the masters of contemplation in the past, and impossible, it seems, but for the divine experience.

While an understanding of the nature of this inner experience is useful, it is perhaps not essential to the further development of theory. At any rate, we return to the logical evolution of the system of norm. We said that the founders of the new model had to presuppose a potential natural order between the impulses which prompted men to desire and to act. It seems inevitable, therefore, that they should first bring these forces to their fold. All the prompting, instinctive forces in human nature they called love, which thus becomes "the first movement of the will and of every appetitive power. . . . Hence in whomsoever there is will and appetite, there must also be love." [8] Accordingly, it is legitimate to say that love manifests itself as desire for objects and activities of manifold nature. It follows that whatever governs men's loves, governs men and the city. In this sense we should understand the

[6] *Ibid.,* p. 2.   [7] *Ibid.,* p. 2.
[8] A. C. Pegis, *Basic Writings of St. Thomas Aquinas* (New York, 1945), vol. I, pp. 215–216.

formula that "love is a uniting and binding force" in society.[9] And as fear—the final binding force in the old city—in order to become operative presupposes the existence of love, ultimately for self, love becomes in the last instance the binding force of all society. We arrive thus at the great formula: "as bodies are moved by gravity, wheresoever they are moved, so souls are moved by love." [10] This discovery is comparable to the much later concept of a physical universe seemingly kept together by a law of gravity. But to this point we may well be followed by the masters of the old city. For it was the insistent habit of loves to attach themselves to the wrong objects that in the last instance necessitated the city of reason, and made the ancients distrustful of emotion. In terms of their city they even had to consider it with hostility. And exactly at this point the full impact of the Christian revolution becomes apparent. Refreshed by new experience St. Augustine continues: "But whether the love that we love them with is to be loved, that is to be declared. It is to be loved." [11]

And all the returned travelers agree with the Augustinian dictum that love is to be loved. And so overwhelming is this conviction that it revolutionizes man's concept of God, and thus of himself and of society. The Christian fathers have agreed with St. John that "God is love." But, then, to love God is to love love, and also to be loved by Him; loving God we love, indeed, the source of the binding and creating force of the city, a force from the beginning poured into each one of us. This love had always been there, but its light was, so to speak, broken in the prism of reason and it governed men by its conversion into fear. And men

[9] Dionysius quoted by St. Thomas, *op. cit.,* p. 215.
[10] St. Augustine, *City of God,* book xi, chap. 27.
[11] *Ibid.,* book xi, chap. 27.

conditioned by the old city—its laws, habits, myths, and beliefs—could not perceive the nature of this love. When the exceptional soul was suddenly liberated from the old illusions and saw the unity of God and man, it was emotionally overwhelmed and deeply changed. This is the source of a new sequence of events, which in importance overshadows the previous work even of genius.

The first impulse of the new man was to project his loves—not on "all the kingdoms of the world . . . and the glory of them," [12] but on God. "For a season" love flows undiverted into God and becomes identified with the binding and creating force of the city. The soul finds its Father, and the sonship involves a participation in His essence. As the Father goes out in creation, so must the son return to the world. The second impulse of the new man is to project his loves back on society. But loves returned have undergone a great metamorphosis. Freed from the many discordant objects of love, they have become united, purified, and strengthened; they have become worthy of the name of Charity; centered not in self, but in God; concerned not with the good of the part but with the good of the whole. They proceed in an orderly fashion ready to promote universal ends; the emotions which set out as a lawless tribe return as a law-abiding nation. Emotion has found a law within itself, a natural order, and, short-circuiting the process of reason, it is on the way to becoming itself norm.

Genius was, either openly or potentially, a resident ruler; the mystic soul is a pilgrim servant. Out of the emotional center of Christianity, there emerged individuals who, in terms of previous experience, represented a new social type, conscious of new func-

[12] *St. Luke,* IV, 5, 6.

tions and exercising a new kind of social influence. The Founder of Christianity tells us little, or nothing, about the inner experience out of which emerged the Son of God. Through ages of intellectualization this process retains its freshness; but, speaking for social theory, we must inquire into its importance for social development.

The wisdom of founders of cities is revealed as much by their silence as by their eloquence. Jesus was conscious of the need of restraint in communication, for: "I have yet many things to say unto you, but ye cannot bear them now." [13] The apparent simplicity of Christian formula and parable cannot hide the complexity of the unsaid; it insists on showing itself in paradox. In order to grasp the meaning of the whole we need an ear for the unsaid. The letter killeth, and it would be intellectual and spiritual suicide to deify the letter of the message rather than the spirit of truth that moves it. The Gospels are valid to the extent they express laws and relationships inherent in the nature of things; but says St. Augustine: "We . . . do not believe in Peter but in Him that Peter believed in. We are edified by Peter's sermons . . . , but not bewitched by his charms nor deceived by his magic. . . . Christ that taught Peter the doctrine of eternal life, teaches us also." [14]

The study of norm led us to consider a group of phenomena which are technically described as the mystical experience. It has been necessary, for a number of reasons, to use terms which were originally theological and which to many have acquired the connotations of the arbitrary, the magical, and the superstitious. The emotional complexes attached to these data render a rational and dispassionate consideration of them difficult. But theory can-

[13] *St. John*, XVI, 12.   [14] St. Augustine, *op. cit.*, book XVIII, chap. 54.

not afford to respect such popular taboos or to like or dislike the data with which it has to deal. The effects of the mystic experience are too important, and too much a chip off that great block called "reality," to be neglected without a falsification of theory. The reason for our concern with these phenomena is plain: it followed from our attempt to find the conditions under which norms (shadows of men's loves) could be thought of as falling in a natural, harmonious order. It was logic that forced us from the purely rational to the emotional aspect of man. So important is a clear and dispassionate understanding, and at the same time so difficult, that the same group of phenomena may usefully be considered from another point of view. Up to the present we have borrowed our concepts chiefly from the Hellenic tradition, and not, as is usual in theology and much of Western political philosophy, from the Hebraic tradition. The latter contained, in fact, inventions and discoveries at which the Hellenic world was only slowly arriving, or which it had grasped only by implication.

It was found that if we were to construct a model process of normative change the primacy had to be in the inner kingdom. This requirement may have had the ring of utopian if the Jews had not already, in their way, been able to realize this great revolution. The Jewish city had its center of gravity in the promise; its projections were in the nature of norm. The Covenant was prior to the founding of the outer kingdom in the land of promise. It lasted after this land was again lost. The obedience to particular habits was not justified by particular myths (though, of course, the system as a whole was not free from the mythical); by and large, the acceptance of particular commands rested on faith in a single god, representing, so to speak, the norm-projection point. The Jews had already demonstrated the practical possibility, and the high survival value, of a city based on the primacy of the inner kingdom. In this light, it is now useful to consider the Christian development.

"Then one of [the Pharisees] which was a lawyer, asked him a question, tempting him, and saying, Master, which is the great commandment in the law? Jesus said unto him, Thou shalt love the Lord thy God with all thy heart, and with all thy soul, and with all thy mind. This is the first and great commandment. And the second is like unto it, Thou shalt love thy neighbor as thyself." [15]

The Founder was born in a city which already required men to project all their loves onto a single screen, and from this screen, so to speak, they were reprojected back to society. But let us try to understand the nature of the reprojection mechanism. It is determined by the nature of Jehovah. He was a high, but at the same time jealous, particularist, and cruel god. This must be so, for a closer examination will show him to be essentially an emanation of tribal reason. Hence, the loves projected onto him were broken, if we may say so, in the prism of reason and returned to the social plane in an infinite number of norms of conduct for all or almost all human activities. But the primacy of reason in the ideal construct could not avoid ending in the changeless. It is true that, like the Aristotelian construct of a perfect city, the Jewish city could not immediately be realized in practice. The faith in Jehovah and the Covenant constituted in actuality a dynamic force of change; it remains nevertheless true that, in the final analysis, the realization of the ideal would result in changeless perfection. But the commands of the law—supported by the love, or rather by the love-converted-into-fear, of God—had a

[15] *St. Matthew*, XXII, 35–39.

strength and a vitality unknown to myth. They were justified by man's relation to God, unshakable by mere temporal upset in habit. The Christian contribution to and development of the Jewish system follows from the new knowledge of God contained in the mystical experience; it does not invalidate existing relationships but builds on their ground: for "God sent not His Son into the world to condemn the world; but that the world through Him might be saved." [16]

When the loves of men are attracted into the love of God, they are not to be shattered by the prism of reason nor to be converted into fears. They should return as love; intellectualization becomes, at the best, a secondary and in itself incidental process. The mastership of the Founder shows itself in economy of teaching. He appeared so unconcerned with the particular forms of social life, so preoccupied with its inner process, that some sincerely believe Him ignorant of the complexities of social living. But looking for what is necessary He proceeds like a physician; He spares His lectures about the functions of the body and prescribes what the patient should do in order to get well. He aims at releasing a process of growth, which in time lets discordant elements fall into harmonious balance. Norm, being the emanation of love, grows according to laws peculiar to itself. And as the common projection point of norm rests in God who is perfect, universal love, He must be thought to be at an infinite distance from the city at the same time as He is present in the city. Hence, the social plan on its journey through time can approach but never reach the projection point of norm. The new concept gives rise to a social dynamism, the end of which reason is unable to perceive.

[16] *St. John,* III, 17.

Indeed, in the terms here employed we would seem to have uncovered, as it were, a pure principle of change—a conclusion already obvious from the position and parentage of norm in the city of reason. But if any city were to be completely carried away by a dynamic impulse, it would dissolve, being launched on "a passage from nothing to nothing." It is literally true that a city cannot see its god and live.

Overwhelming as the pilgrim instinct of the mystic soul may appear, the founder of a new city cannot forget the limiting conditions of social growth. To prevent chaos and disintegration there must be a principle regulating the rate of change, so that through it all the necessary social functions remain bounded in value. Hence, in actual life (as opposed to a pure model) social growth becomes somewhat of a compromise or, if you like, a marriage between the static and the dynamic, between justice and myth on the one hand and love and norm on the other. How this compromise is to be effected presents theoretically the crucial problem of the new departure. It requires us to describe how the reprojected impulses of love shall be ordered into a socially operative system of norm and gradual change. And the Founder gave the world a formula; it speaks with authority provocative of echoes; resting on a tower of complexity, it is understood by all:

"Therefore all things whatsoever ye would that men should do to you, do ye even so to them. . . ." [17]

[17] *St. Matthew*, VII, 12.

15

A C I T Y
Sighted in Hope

OUR SAVIOUR'S GREAT RULE, THAT 'WE SHOULD LOVE
OUR NEIGHBOURS AS OURSELVES' IS SUCH A
FUNDAMENTAL TRUTH FOR THE REGULATING OF
HUMAN SOCIETY, THAT I THINK BY THAT ALONE
ONE MIGHT WITHOUT DIFFICULTY DETERMINE
ALL THE CASES AND DOUBTS IN SOCIAL MORALITY.

—John Locke [1]

BEFORE WE CONSIDER THE APPLICATION of the principle of norm-
formation itself, it may be useful to recapitulate the general problem of norm from another side. Imagine, therefore, an organism
composed of interdependent cells in dynamic equilibrium. The
cells respond to given stimuli with given responses, and behave as
if they were joined together in a system of habit. The observer
cannot know what goes on inside the cells, or why they behave
as they do. But considering their behavior he is free to deduce in
them certain characters which can be used in a gradual formulation
of hypotheses, theory, or "law." Such generalizations are useful in
so far as they interpret experience meaningfully and, pragmatically

[1] "Conduct of the Understanding," *The Works of John Locke* (ed. J. A. St.
John), London, 1883, 1, 34. Relevant passages in "An Essay Concerning Human Understanding" refer, instead of to the second great commandment, to
the Golden Rule, which may appropriately be read into the quotation above.

speaking, give us manipulative advantages. This first illustration shows a situation roughly comparable to that of men in a hypothetical state of nature.

We imagine next that the individual cells become endowed by their creator with reason. They acquire the capability of considering means to an end and thus of choice, i.e., a faculty of acting or not acting in response to certain stimuli. The awakened cell would become conscious of itself as an entity; it would begin to feel itself subject to the pulls and pressures of outside forces. Aware of its own impulses on the one hand, and the demands emanating from the system as a whole on the other hand, it would, no doubt, begin to conceive the later as hostile and arbitrary forces. And as the outside impulses could not meet the criteria of private intelligence, the cell would resist them: the system would slow down, become confused and, after a point, disintegrate. Hence, the survival of the organism, and indirectly that of each cell, demands a reform which neutralizes the centrifugal force of self-centered reason. This figure illustrates the situation when the city is on the verge of emerging out of nature. We imagine further, then, that some cell, or cells, conceive (or act as if they conceived) that the outside force was really necessity pertaining to the life of the whole of which each formed a part. Obedience to the outside impulse would be conceived as a common condition of survival. Cells must acquire notions (or act as if they did) of the common necessity; they must be induced to meet their functions, and if possible, with the same lack of resistance as in a state of nature. As reason is a permanent addition to the system, it would become necessary to short-circuit its disruptive tendency, and to obtain the voluntary assent of the cells to the social functions, a consent to be obtained by interposing between the cell and the system a counterfeited experience. Through this arrangement the force of self-consciousness is tricked into the belief that in pursuing social ends it is really pursuing private ends. This figure illustrates roughly the previous construct of the city of reason.

While the hypothetical state of nature represented a stable equilibrium, that of the city was unstable. It rested on the mechanism of short-circuiting reason, and could be maintained only as long as this short-circuit was not broken. But the system of myth was brittle and could be disrupted by outside shock. The static character of the city was, in the last analysis, traceable to this brittleness of myth. Hence, looking for a continuous process of social change, it became logical to ask: Is it possible to find a stable, though dynamic, equilibrium in a system composed of reasonable beings? If we are to remove myth, is it not obvious that we must first find a new way of preventing the release of the centrifugal tendencies of self-consciousness?

Myth and theory agreed that man's rise out of nature was mixed up with the dawn of self-consciousness. Social theory is not able to explain why, or how, the self-conscious human entity appeared on the stage. Such an entity represents to us a social datum (as creation is a datum of theology), and attempts to explain it and to break it down into simpler elements lead further into the unknown and finally to a disintegration of social experience itself. Similarly, if during the course of history, a new human entity should develop, social theory ought to acknowledge, even if it could not explain, such an occurrence. It should, accepting it as a datum, find a place for it in theory. It was not without reason that we emphasized in the foregoing the mystical experience. We are aware that dealing with this subject we may have touched off strong emotional reactions; but these reactions themselves are significant by indicating the presence of some vital nerve. We are close to phenomena which appear comparable to the emergence of a self-conscious entity: or rather, out of the mystical experience is born a new kind of man who enters the stream of social events and becomes a datum; the pattern of theory can never return to what it was before.

The Stoics and the Neo-Platonists realized that the world-city required universal virtue of a new kind. But the construct of reason created emotional conflict which reason could hide but not resolve. In order to straighten out the emotions, intervention on the emotional plane was required. And the mystical experience supplies such an emotional reorientation. The new man becomes an entity endowed with universal consciousness; he becomes as different from the self-conscious man as the self-conscious man would be from an unconscious or natural man. And it was as difficult to explain to the still self-conscious man what the universal consciousness implies as it is to explain to a child what it is like to be a grown-up. For definition of a whole emotional state is, without experience, almost meaningless. Let it be said nonetheless that the new man is lifted out of self and feels, and not only knows, himself to be a part of the whole. And as it is natural for the self-conscious man to find his end in self, so is it natural for the new man to find his end in the life of the whole. Rather than trying to sharpen this definition, consider a system of ideas into which the universally conscious man has already entered as a familiar element.

According to John Stuart Mill the *summum bonum* of society is contained in the Greatest Happiness Principle which "holds that actions are right in proportion as they tend to promote happiness, wrong as they tend to produce the reverse of happiness. By happiness is intended pleasure, and absence of pain, by unhappiness pain, and the privation of pleasure." [2] According to this criterion a perfect city would be so arranged as to permit the realization of maximum pleasure. Simple as this statement may appear, the hedonistic constructs have given rise to many misunderstandings. In order to clear the ground, let it be understood that pleasure and pain are subjective phenomena, and that they as such are incapable of measurement, summation, and statistical manipulation. The hedonistic philosophy remains contradictory, if not meaningless, as long as, lured away by individualist preoccupations, we try to manipulate quantities of pleasure and pain. But the situation changes when we consider society as a whole. For by definition all men are in pursuit of some object of love, and any object of love in the pursuit appears good. Whatever moralists may have said, saint and sinner are distinguished by the object of their loves, not by the ability of the former to withdraw himself from the gravitational force of pleasure and pain. And as happiness results when men move freely in the pursuit of their loves, it follows also by definition, that total maximum hedonistic satisfaction is realized (assuming at least that anticipated and realized pleasures are the same) in a society where all men can freely pursue their loves. In the absence of compulsion and frustration men would be free, requiring neither rulers nor the opium of myth to perform their work. By definition each man would do what he liked. Supposing that the hedonistic assumptions were compatible with social balance, one would, in fact, have arrived at a new stable (though not static) equilibrium in society.

[2] John Stuart Mill, *Utilitarianism, Liberty and Representative Government,* Everyman's Library, p. 6.

But no hedonist was quite as naive as to confuse the ideal construct with reality. It may have represented a goal worthy of being striven for, but they knew that men, as actually constituted, could not be entrusted with complete liberty without throwing society into anarchy. They asked, therefore, by what means society could approach the ideal position. They answered that liberty required that the objects of men's loves be first arranged in patterns compatible with social balance. In the present world, they said, men should not seek to maximize their own pleasure, but seek "the greatest amount of pleasure altogether . . . [and] utilitarianism, therefore, could only attain its end by the general cultivation of nobleness of character, even if each individual were only benefited by the nobleness of others, and his own, so far as happiness is concerned, were a sheer deduction from the benefit." [3] The hedonists were returned, therefore, to the Aristotelian preoccupation with virtue as being a necessary condition for a true union of citizens. In order to realize the good life it is essential to create a human character which voluntarily, or at least without resistance, tends to act in a way that promotes the common weal. The problems, now couched in terms of the Greatest Happiness Principle, are far from new; but the solutions suggested are not without novelty. Like Aristotle, Mill depends on a process of character-formation, and goes on to ask how the will—that censor of human impulse—can be taught to admit good actions and suppress bad actions. This, of course, again raises the familiar questions of right action and of how virtue can be instilled in the citizens.

In determining virtue-content Aristotle referred to preconceived systems of habit, or constitutions. Mill, on the other hand, did not attempt to catalogue virtues appropriate to different cities. He con-

[3] *Ibid.,* pp. 10–11.

ceived virtue as a gradually developing order between the loves themselves, centered in emotion to which intellectualization had to be considered as secondary. He provided a principle of norm-formation, for "in the golden rule of Jesus of Nazareth, we read the complete spirit of the ethics of utility." [4] Considering the process of character-formation Mill then continues: "As the means of making the nearest approach to this ideal, utility would enjoin first, that laws and social arrangements should place happiness, of every individual, as nearly as possible in harmony with the interest of the whole; and secondly that education and opinion . . . should use [their] power to establish in the mind of every individual an indissoluble association between his own happiness and the good of the whole." [5] It seems then that the realization of natural order in society is possible only by the education of the emotions in a new feeling. The "indissoluble association" between the individual happiness and the common good, presupposes indeed "the feeling of unity with our fellow-creatures . . . what it cannot be denied that Christ intended it to be." [6] The ancients let reason preside over virtue-formation; Mill now lets the intellectualization of virtue follow from a primary emotion. The construct of the ancients presupposed the universality of the self-conscious man; the new construct presupposed the possibility of developing the universally conscious man. Mill, therefore, took the reality and further potentiality of universal consciousness for granted.

It has now become apparent why we have undertaken this excursion into utilitarianism. It supplies ready-made, and as an integral part of theoretical tradition, the final stage towards which our simile has been driving. The process of bounded, gradual

[4] *Ibid.,* p. 16.   [5] *Ibid.,* p. 16.   [6] *Ibid.,* p. 25.

change in society becomes feasible when men, arranging themselves, like cells in an organism, follow their emotional impe-
tus, not as self-contained entities but as conscious members of
the whole. The final stage of social development seems to lead
to a construct, which on a higher and conscious level, reproduces
the kind of stable, unitarian equilibrium that we found in the
state of nature. It is characterized by liberty in the outer kingdom,
and obedience to the law contained in the universal consciousness
in the inner kingdom.

Therefore, in order to provide for bounded social growth of the
evolutionary pattern, one must presuppose a spread of universal
consciousness. This force made its appearance on a modest scale,
manifested to start with in some single soul. The new movement
appeared as potentiality, and its realization was contingent on the
possibility of, so to speak, emotional contagion. And to the extent
such a spread takes place, it is inevitable that the new city should
create a new division between men. There is a category of men
living in the many cities and classes of the world according to
self, or as the fathers would say, the "flesh." To this is added another category of men who live according to the good of the whole,
or as the fathers would say the "spirit." This great divide, of course,
would fade away if all should become converted to the ways of
the new city. But whatever the ultimate outcome of events may
turn out to be, the process of conversion is a millenary one, and it
is necessary to foresee a long period of conflict and transition.
These meetings and fusions between the two great concepts of
society offer problems of utmost importance and complexity. To
deal with them is an object of the present book as a whole. But
in order to do so it is necessary to have some idea of the inherent
nature of the new process, just as we needed a picture of the

nature of the old city. Hence, while the task is almost impossible, we have no other way than to attempt to conceive of a pure process of social change. In order to construct such a model we have to grant it the condition it tries to realize. Seek to imagine, therefore, that we have reached a state in which the universal consciousness has already supplanted self-consciousness.

The individual would feel like a cell trying to function for the good of the whole. In a system of this nature the health of the whole would depend upon the health of each part, just as the health of the part would depend on the health of the whole. The part would seem to live and have its being in the whole and give itself up to it. But in so doing it would, in fact, acquire a value greater than before; for the harmony and perfection of the whole could now be disturbed by the imperfection of disobedience of a single person. And so intense has the vision of such a state become that it has inspired a knowledge of the dignity and immeasurable value of man. The illumination of the vision has penetrated the darkness around the nucleus in which it had its birth, and continues to have its true home.

In men guided by the impulses of universal consciousness, and thus in theological language obedient to the will of God, there could be no conflict between private and public interest. And if we remember how basic this conflict was to the emergence and construction of the old city, it is easy to perceive that its removal will have far-reaching consequences. To start with it would make away with the need for myth. Men could look at reality without the vision becoming blended with the interposed pattern of counterfeited experience. It would be possible to follow the pursuit of truth and the inherent powers of reason would have occasion to change man's knowledge and man's ways of doing things. Truth makes men free, but such freedom is possible only when the conditions for freedom are already realized. And if voluntary assent to habit is already there (habit being in such a state but emotion realized), it follows that there is no need of imposing habit. Hence, the mechanisms of order, in the old meaning, would become obsolete and could be abolished. But the consequences carry us into still more essential relationships. The hierarchically stratified structure of the old city rested on transfer feeding the superstructure needed to perform a number of social functions. But if social balance should result from the spontaneous behavior of a union of citizens, the need of imposed transfer would cease. With the changes now observed, the whole justification of vertical integration in society would have vanished. The wound left by the division of the city would heal; the determination of transfer, the distribution of income and property would become incidental to social life rather than its determinant. The need for wise use of the social surplus would not disappear, but it would assume the character of a social trust to be used in ways most conducive to the common welfare. Hence, to the extent that the city of love is able to establish itself, there can "be no more two nations, neither [can] they be divided into two kingdoms, any more at all." [7]

The tie that bound the new order to the realities of life on earth was the principle of norm-formation. It directs universal force to universal ends. Whenever it starts to operate it tends to employ similar means for similar ends. Societies formed by it, while not necessarily alike, tend to assume some basic similarities. With the disappearance of separate upper kingdoms, particularism loses its natural habitat, and there ceases to be another. Feeling

[7] *Ezekiel,* xxxvii, 22.

themselves as members of a common order, they have reason to welcome, and not oppose, such union of territorial units as technical developments render possible and desirable. The preëxistence of a common inner kingdom creates a brotherhood which renders war as unthinkable as it had already rendered its instrument, the state, obsolete. Men can be habituated in the ways of peace instead of those of war. Peace—being the universal agreement of the order of loves—would become something real, and not merely a temporary armistice between nations which necessity had made enemies.

The projection of a society ruled by universal consciousness thus carries us a small way into the future. The ultimate results of the processes released lose themselves in the unknowable. But it is not without significance that the first stages on the way have been seen, in almost the same general outline, by all masters of the Western tradition touched by the wing of the universal. Contemplating the "final peace" of the new city, St. Augustine summarizes what all have more or less perfectly seen: "We shall have no need of reason to rule over sin, for there shall be no sin at all there, but God shall rule men, and the soul the body; and obedience shall there be as pleasant and easy, as the state of them that live shall be glorious and happy." [8] And no seer of the vision has imagined that the disappearance of imposed order, states, rulers, and war would mean absence of social life. The road to a more abundant life is seen as dotted with a variety of voluntary associations serving common purposes. Ideas have a way of institutionalizing themselves, but associations and institutions would have to be born, change, or die as the city grew, as new inventions were made, as new needs arose, and as men progressed in moral

[8] *City of God,* book xix, chap. 27.

grandeur. It would be without meaning, therefore, to try to visualize the exact institutional framework of a city in the process of continuous growth.

The development of new patterns rests on the presence of a new concept of leadership. In a simple society it may seem relatively easy to translate the principle of norm-formation into action and practical rules of behavior, manners, and attitudes. But the more society grows—and the dynamic impulses resulting from the liberation of reason can be assumed as progressively more potent—the more delicate does the question of application become. Hence arises the need for moral leadership. This is a need to which we shall return. It suffices to say here that such leadership has to be voluntarily accepted, and that it has to be based on confidence in the leaders' wisdom, knowledge, and good will. While the new city has no place for rulers, it cannot exist without the selfless service of wise advisers; for in it *imperare nihil aliud est quam consulere.*

The Christian visions of the advent of a millennium are subject to a previous realization of universal consciousness. It represents an order that is potential in the advent of the kingdom of God, and in it only. It demands effort to be realized. The conditions of realization will be considered later; meanwhile, recall that the Christian vision of the future state of man seems to meet a deep need. Once the bright images have been cast on the dark screen of an old city, they create a lasting unrest in man's mind. They become a focus of longing and aspiration. Gradually, in forms ever more foreign to the conditional nature of the genuine vision, they assume the nature of a secondary acting force. They lead to hopes which demand realization in the narrow framework of self-consciousness. Mistaking the original emotional impulse that gave them birth, they generate in their turn a kind of "enthusiasm which spreads from soul to soul, unceasingly, like a conflagration," [9] until there seems to be no great contemporary movement which has not directly or indirectly, wholly or partially, drawn its inspiration from the original vision. There is a tragic wistfulness about these spreading echoes, a violence and a fanaticism foreign to the life of love. But, as we listen to the words of another founder of state, it is impossible for us not to recognize in them an authentic echo of the first voice. There will come a time, Marx says, by necessity, when the state "becomes really representative of society as a whole, [and] makes itself superfluous. As soon as there is no longer any class in society to be held in subjection . . . there is nothing more to be repressed which would make a repressive force, a State, necessary. The first act in which the State really comes forward as the representative of society as a whole . . . is at the same time its last independent act as a state. The interference of the state power in social relations becomes superfluous in one sphere after another, and then, ceases of itself. . . . The state is not abolished, *it withers away*." [10]

[9] Bergson, *The Two Sources of Morality and Religion,* p. 52.
[10] *Anti-Dühring,* p. 308–309.

16

A CITY

That Tames Lust

> BUT I SEE ANOTHER LAW IN MY MEMBERS,
> WARRING AGAINST THE LAW OF MY MIND, AND
> BRINGING ME INTO CAPTIVITY TO THE LAW OF SIN
> WHICH IS IN MY MEMBERS. O WRETCHED MAN
> THAT I AM! WHO SHALL DELIVER ME FROM THE
> BODY OF THIS DEATH?—*St. Paul* [1]

IN THE CITY OF REASON the threat of social disintegration was felt
to result from the difficulty of satisfying the functions of order and
defense. In spite of all the safeguards, imposed by rulers and
legislators, cycles of social change tended, in the long run, to provoke an unlimited, and therefore destructive, expansion of one
or both of these functions. In order to combine social change with
continuous social balance it would seem desirable, then, to eliminate these functions, or more precisely, to remove what rendered
them necessary. And recalling the inherent tendencies of a city
governed by love, we found that this is exactly what would happen if we were able to convert the city from myth to norm, and
let the inner kingdom assume the primacy over the outer. At the
end of a general conversion of men to the new ways, social balance
would have become reduced to a relationship between production

[1] *Romans*, VII, 23–24.

and reproduction, and such secondary functions as the stage of integration reached would necessitate. Hence, while the relationships between production and reproduction were basic in the old city, they acquire an ever greater significance in the new. And before we can logically proceed to discuss the ways in which the new city can be made to conquer the old, we seem obliged to inquire whether or not a population balance, compatible with the purpose of the new city, is theoretically conceivable.

The primacy that the natural family accorded to the reproductive function was the cornerstone upon which the vertical integration of cities rested. From this primacy the institutions of transfer were derived, the superstructures of states and churches, the need for habit-supporting myth, and also the inner tensions which rendered balance so vulnerable to change. And we agreed that as long as the family continued to breed regardless of consequence, so long would the removal of imposed transfer return the city—via anarchy and violent population contractions—to a state of nature. Lasting social life whether on the vertical or the horizontal model presupposes, therefore, a social surplus sufficient to meet the requirements of other social functions. In the horizontal model this implies the necessity of finding some means, other than imposed transfer, to prevent population growth from absorbing all surplus. We deal in this chapter with long-time relationships: the problem naturally presents a different aspect under the short or medium term. In existing cities the full effects of certain tendencies may take generations, and even centuries, to make themselves felt. The effects of population growth may for a time be obscured, and apparently reversed, by intervention of more temporary factors such as increases in labor productivity, discoveries of new land, or higher incidence of mortality due to epidemics and similar

causes. If economic progress were automatic and always proceeded at a rate commensurate with potential population increase,
the population problem would not be intelligible. But as, in fact,
any continuous population increase would, in the end, require
more than finite economic space, such dreams can be discarded
here.

Many citizens of the new city have taken an ambiguous position on the basic issue now raised. Some seem sincerely to have
believed that general poverty is the only state compatible with
a good society. But the problem is dealt with by the Founder in
several parables, the most illuminating being perhaps that of a
certain rich man. When he asked what he must do in order to
inherit eternal life, the Master told him to sell what he had and
give it to the poor; for riches, in the old city, were the fruits
of transfer, and as the new city would tend to the abolition of
imposed transfer, the new man could not base his life upon this
institution. And as the abolition of transfer would lead to disintegration of the old city, it would be impossible for a man, so
long as he remained within the framework of the old city, to give
away what he had. The re-transfer implied in the parable becomes
possible only when a man inwardly has become a full member
of the new inner kingdom. With the old "men it is impossible,
but not with God: for with God all things are possible." [2]

But it would be unwarranted then to imagine that the abolition
of imposed transfer implied also a condemnation of surplus as
such. The Founder never tired of reminding his followers to feed
the hungry, to clothe the naked, to visit the sick; indeed, from the
first, the miracles of the new city consisted in giving wine to the
joyful, bread to the hungry, aid to the sick, and life to those who

[2] *St. Mark,* x, 27.

were dead. And as these works require the use of social surplus, the new city requires only that the method of its procurement, and the principles of its use, should become subject to its own law.

In a state of nature there could exist no socially conditioned conflict between men's impulses. Such conflict was contained in self-consciousness which entered on the stage simultaneously with the city. While in any city of reason the continuance of the natural birth rate gives rise to phenomena later considered as nondesirable, this rate remains the cornerstone of imposed order. It was inevitable that rulers and mythmakers should combine in giving particular care to safeguards protecting the primacy of the reproductive function in the lower kingdoms. To attack habits serving this purpose, or to doubt myths supporting them, would be sacrilege. Hence, prudent "stewards of the mysteries of God" [3] would take into account the dangers of attacking the old city on a point so sensitive. They would, if possible, employ the oblique approach, and affect human behavior in the name of some general appeal. The Founder, reserving the "mysteries of the kingdom of heaven" for those who were able to perceive them in implication, and thus wise enough to impose restraints upon themselves, protected the tender growths of the new city from premature exposure; and incidentally He thereby also protected the old city from premature dissolution. For we have seen that the voluntary limitation of births in the multitude represents a potential weapon powerful enough to nullify transfer and thus to disestablish rule. But to destroy the "peace and order" of the old city before the new city has grown strong enough to substitute its own would, in fact, kill also the new city. It is not difficult to perceive, then, that many

[3] 1 *Corinthians,* IV, 1.

circumstances conspire, preventing the ten thousand instructors in Christ from sharing the potent insights of the fathers. It is natural—and within limits expedient—that the popular instructors should share the values of the cities in which they happen to be born. The theologian's regard for the letter of the Hebraic law has provided further means of rationalizing old social tenets in supposedly Christian terms, even when they are obviously foreign to the spirit of Christianity.

If men live long enough in any closed city, they will come to consider the values, dictated by its particular necessity, as absolute and universal. But if a process of social growth exists, and if several different cities are thrown into contact with each other, there will come a period when the naive value-absolutism dissolves and is followed by an equally naive value-relativism. The observer, of course, will have discovered that values are different, but he would be mistaken in the belief that they are arbitrary or subjective phenomena. While, no doubt, in the matter of form they leave room for many subjective elements, their content is determined by the objective necessities of social balance. And when the new city opens up the vista of a new social potentiality, it introduces beyond norms, adapted to particular societies and their shifting circumstance and degree of development, an objectively given standard of valuation—a "measure of the rule which God hath distributed" [4]—according to which a particular norm is to be judged. While the old system of valuation holds good within the sphere of its own assumptions, the new city, based on fresh assumptions, brings about a revolution in traditional values. In the old city that was good which tended to protect its life, so in the new city that is good which tends to promote a life more abundant.

[4] 2 *Corinthians*, x, 13.

"Sin," in the sense of the actual, is what frustrates the new ends and leads to social death.

Hence, bearing these relationships in mind, it is obvious that given valuations as to "good" and "evil" in a city tell us a great deal about the underlying standard of valuations, and the nature of the explicit or implicit social construction they represent. And considering the reticence of founders of cities, and the expediently restricted views of a popular priesthood, it becomes desirable, if not necessary, to consider the new teachings of "sin" so as to reconstruct the underlying ideas of basic social relationships. In order, more particularly, to study the new concepts of the right relationship between the functions of production and reproduction, we are led to consider the concept of "original sin." It is true that theological concepts have ceased to be respectable subjects of intellectual analysis. Still, being social data, having influenced men's behavior, a theorist cannot afford to let preconceived notions as to their nature prevent him from including them in his analysis. A psychologist may not "believe" in dreams, but he has to deal with them as data of theory.

Now, the new city did not arise out of nature, but out of the old city. And as the first city carried with it the heritage from nature, so does the new carry with it the heritage from the old city directly, and from nature indirectly. And, says the Apostle, as "The first man is of the earth, earthy . . . we have borne the image of the earthy." [5] For when the city emerged, it took hold of human nature, molding in it the forms of a "first man." The double pull of obligation and belief dragged him along the road of what was then necessity. The voice of conscience (and we mean the categorical imperative, the loud Kantian opponent to the still

[5] I *Corinthians,* xv, 47, 49.

Socratic voice) prevented forward movement; and it is difficult
to overestimate this force which generation upon generation
stamped man's character with an identical "image" of necessity.
It is to the credit of the speculative genius of the West to have
been able to maintain a distinction between this "image" on the
one hand, and human nature as such on the other. The fathers
of the new city conceived "good" and "evil" in social terms;
human nature in a pure form, being, if found at all, in a state of
nature, innocent. What in cities appears as "evil" is not due to
the "evilness" of human nature, but to imperfection in character-
formation. For, says the Great Doctor: "Hear them not that
praise the fire's light and dispraise the heat, respecting not the
nature of it but their own profit and disprofit. They would see,
but they would not burn. But they consider not that this light
they like so, being immoderately used, hurts a tender eye." [6] He
continues, "wherefore all natures are good, because they have
their form, kind, and a certain harmony withal in themselves." [7]
This inherent goodness extends to the body, the needs, desires
and appetites thereof, for: "if any man say that the flesh is cause
of the viciousness of the soul, he is ignorant of man's nature, for
the corruptible body does not burden the soul. . . . We are . . .
burdened with this corruptible body, and yet knowing that it is
not the body's nature, but corruption, that causes this burden." [8]

The key concept of "corruption" goes back to Paul. Corruption
literally implies nothing else than the familiar term of disintegration or, in a wider sense, death. "Evil" then becomes a kind of
disorder in an inherently and potentially good system of relationships, exactly as "corruption . . . is the punishment of the

[6] St. Augustine, *City of God,* book xii, chap. 4.
[7] *Ibid.,* book xii, chap. 5.   [8] *Ibid.,* book xiv, chap. 3.

first sin, not the cause. The corruptible flesh made not the soul to sin, but the sinning soul made the flesh corruptible. . . . For man became like the devil not in being in the flesh (for so was not the devil) but in living according to his own lust, that is, according to the fleshly man." [9] Translating these venerable terms into our own, they imply that the "fall of man" derives from the rise of self-consciousness. This first event gave rise to the social situation represented by the old city. To live according to the "flesh"—or in emotion centered in self—is both a cause and an effect of the city; it is inseparable from the tendency of disintegration inherent in that construct. This situation is necessary in terms of the old city, and thus in a sense "good." But it becomes "evil" to the extent that there is presented an alternative which is more life-promoting. And compared with the new prespectives opened up with universal consciousness—in which emotion is centered on the whole—the life according to the "flesh" will appear as "sin." The fall of man, and the complementary concept of "original sin," represent then nothing else than the rise of self-consciousness, and the consequent rise of a city of reason inherently subject to disintegration. And as social life arose out of this first event, so is the "corruption" inherent in this life traceable as a consequence of (or the "punishment" for) the same event. The children of the first parents and their children's children are born into, live and die in, an environment which predestines them to repeat, with only slight variation, a basic pattern. But this compulsion is not easy to discover for men who live altogether captive in it. And as they are endowed with reason they must, in their own estimation, retain a faculty of choice. The will goes on saying its yea and its nay. In private terms the problem of social good and of

[9] *Ibid.,* book xiv, chap. 3.

social evil comes to present itself primarily as a problem of the will. In this sense, the "cause" of evil appears as the "assent of the will to vicious desire." [10]

But it would be dangerous to pursue the analysis on a subjective basis. The search for ultimate causes of social events in the realm of individual psychology leads to infinite regression, and we should in moral judgment look forward to consequence rather than backwards to "cause." "It is not the thing to which we fall . . . that is evil: that is, we fall to no evil natures, but against nature's order, from the highest to the lower. Herein is evil." [11] And in order to understand "vicious desire" we are returned to desire in general. Lust, then "is the general name given to all desires." [12] They seek objects which are good in themselves, and corruption is the consequence of disorder in the hierarchy of loves. The inherent corruptness of the old city can then be expressed as consequence of the wrong order of its loves, and the many conflicts caused by this wrongness. But, it would, as we have seen, be a mistake, considering the problem socially rather than individually, to assume that the apparent "disorder" of loves in the old city was withdrawn from law. Individually speaking, the conflict, becoming conscious on the level of will, may appear so; but in fact these conflicts, these disorders, are subject to lawful sequences. It is natural, perhaps, to imagine that what appears subjectively harmonious and beneficial is lawful and what appears violent and destructive is lawless. But a storm, an earthquake, and an explosion are, in fact, as lawful as the rise and fall of day, and to be explained only in terms of law sufficiently general to admit all observed phenomena whether they imply integration or dis-

[10] *Ibid.*, book XII, chap. 7.   [11] *Ibid.*, book XII, chap. 8.
[12] *Ibid.*, book XIV, chap. 4.

integration. And so with lust in the old city. The sequences of loves, dictated by self, tend to repeat themselves in endless series. And "although . . . there be many lusts, yet when we read the word 'lust' alone, without mention of the object, we commonly take it for the unclean motion of the generative parts." [13] In a natural man, observation often suggests the presence of an almost overwhelming pressure of desire attaching itself to objects and activities pertaining to the reproductive function. This pressure, considering the structure of the city, must be, if not socially induced, at least socially conditioned and maintained. It does not necessarily pertain to human nature itself, but to that human character created by cities. But, continues St. Augustine: "What wise and godly man is there, who being married, and knowing, as the apostle says, 'how to possess his vessel in holiness and honour, and not in the lust of concupiscence, as the Gentiles do, which know not God,' had not rather (if he could) beget his children without this lust, that his members might obey his mind in this act of propagation, as his other members in fulfilling their particular functions, and be ruled by his will, not compelled by concupiscence?" [14]

We do not wish to get lost in disputations as to the use and misuse of the concept of "original sin." It suffices here to retain the broad original sense in which it implies a lusting for any object, or objects, outside the order of love and reason, and that, more particularly, this disorder has become intimately connected with the reproductive function. But the concept of sin is logically nothing else than the shadow of a good; in the positive sense, therefore, the good for which the fathers primarily strove was a bringing of the reproductive function under the dominion of love-

[13] *Ibid.,* book xiv, chap. 16.   [14] *Ibid.,* book xiv, chap. 16.

enlightened reason or, if you like, the institution of a normatively regulated birth-rate. How reproductive norms can be formed is to be considered; but before we move into the field of positive theory, there remain certain aspects which touch upon the liberation of man from his ancient bondage to lust.

We have repeated, perhaps too often, that social life implies the molding of human nature into certain forms of character. Men born into the city cannot avoid, therefore, having stamped upon them what the apostle calls an "image of the earthy." Thus stamped by social necessity and incorporated into the social system, the individual becomes subject to the categorical imperatives of ancient obligation and belief. These two backward pulls represent the same force that the Apostle describes as the "law of our members." And when a new man is born in the dawn of universal consciousness, and thus feels the impulse of forming in himself a new character, living according to "the law of our mind," he becomes, as it were, the battlefield of two opposing forces. When men seek to be "transformed by the renewing of [their] mind," [15] there comes a crucial moment when the fate of the new city hangs in the balance. To all appearances we meet a private conflict; we observe men who seem either unwilling to adjust or incapable of adjusting themselves to environment. On the one hand, then, they cannot help feeling, on a higher level of consciousness, the pull of the ancient obligations, and on the other the call of one as yet untried by experience: "For I was alive without the law once; but when the commandment came, sin revived, and I died. And the commandment which was ordained to life, I found to be unto death." [16]

We observed that when in the final stages of the old civilization

[15] *Romans,* XII, 2.   [16] *Romans,* VII, 9–10.

universalism became an acute issue, disintegration had already
set in. When virtue is ebbing, rulers have little choice but to
divert energies into channels least harmful to order. Nothing
will appear safer or simpler than disarming potential discontent
by a stimulus given to the senses. And we found that now the
Great Mother showed herself double-faced. The worship of fertility degenerates into the unusual, the unnatural, and the cruel,
for to a mature sensualist death becomes a final exciter. But the
new man, living on a high plane of sensibility, is perhaps more
conscious of the dark attraction of *Libido* than the old man dulled
by habit. She reveals herself in new enticing shapes. The private
mind which has to endure the conflict between the highly potent
images of the old world, and the nascent images of the new, is
exposed to a tension of, we are inclined to believe, unique intensity. The danger of this encounter, and the deep hurt it leaves
behind, is difficult to appreciate for generations which have been
able to profit from the victories of those who have gone before. If
the pioneers had succumbed in the first battle of liberation (which
was not, as is often supposed, a battle between body and soul), the
new city could not have survived. But after each victory the powers
of the Great Mother tend to decrease. A victorious, or partly victorious, generation incorporates some of its gains into the surviving system of habit and belief. These gains become protected
by the great conservation-mechanisms, and the voice to which
the multitude listens is mixed up with echoes leading back to the
new voice. While habit and belief may not pull men forward,
they tend to drag them back with less force.

Whenever the new city has moved forward, it has become involved anew in this original conflict. It takes on an ascetic and
puritanical aspect. This discipline is a means to an end; it is to

be likened to the discipline that athletes impose upon themselves. And when the new city ceases to advance—and even more when it retreats before the resurgent old city—the discipline seems to become meaningless. But the relationship between the Great Mother and the old city is mutual. Her worship makes men "slaves to sin," and subjects them to the necessity out of which the city of reason grew. Hence, when we observe her worship return, it is a warning that the outer kingdom is on the way to reverting to its original position. The ancients were led to the altar of the Great Mother by necessity; but we "have no cloak for [our] sin." [17]

[17] *St. John,* xv, 22.

17

A CITY
Creating New Order

.

VERILY I SAY UNTO YOU, WHERESOEVER THIS GOSPEL
SHALL BE PREACHED IN THE WHOLE WORLD,
THERE SHALL ALSO THIS THAT THIS WOMAN HATH
DONE BE TOLD FOR A MEMORIAL OF HER.[1]

IN ORDER TO CREATE THE CONDITIONS needed for new social order,
means had to be found of lessening the pressure of population.
The concept of "original sin" negatively opposed the "natural"
rate of births and aimed positively at incorporating the reproductive function in a general order of loves. The fathers of the new
city have not received the credit due to them as discoverers of the
relationship between social order and reproduction; they have
rather been censured for their distrust of the Great Mother and
are said to have deprived men of the pleasant and healthy outlets
which are granted to her worshipers. Still, the fathers undertook
a great task and, if they were to succeed, they had to proceed with
vigor. It is easier for the spectator than for the combatant to
weigh carefully each act and each word.

Let it be assumed now that they have overcome the Great
Mother. They would have succeeded in undermining the city of
reason; they would have opened the way for new order, but it

[1] *St. Matthew,* XXVI, 13.

remains to be seen whether or not they would be able to establish enduring social balance, which is primarily an equilibrium between the economic and demographic functions. This question carries over to a consideration of the norm-formation mechanism in a special but crucial instance. And as the new city in essence represents a process of change, it cannot, like the old city, be visualized in the form of a static model. In order to communicate notions as to the relationships involved, it is necessary to envisage the new city at the point where it, so to speak, breaks into an already existing city. It is inevitable that the form of this encounter will be influenced by shifting circumstance, but underlying all variation there are some principles of general validity.

The new city rescues man from "the torrent of human habit," [2] but it cannot free him from "human want." Tied down by these wants the old city had, in the last instance, to give priority to the reproductive function, and thus to render woman subservient to this function. And so powerful were these "stern and lasting necessities" that the ancient notions of woman's place in society persisted, even if in modified form, among some of the fathers of Christianity. Paul, in particular, has supplied the authority to lesser instructors who have preached the "natural" subordination of women. It is no wonder then that great multitudes and many rulers go on believing it to be a woman's first duty to take her place uncomplainingly in the ancient race between birth and death, so saving, it is said, both the family and the city. But necessary as such arrangements may have been under the old assumptions, they exacted a price the new city cannot pay. Woman had to be trained for her role from infancy. The family came to imitate the imposed order of the city; man became a little ruler lording it

[2] St. Augustine, *Confessions,* I. XVI, 25.

over a multitude of women, children, and slaves. And one generation of women—with a cruelty particular to the oppressed—
trained the following in submission. It is significant, then, that
the Founder himself when approached by his Mother (who, in
so much, came to resemble a tender version of the Great Mother)
used harsh words, saying: "Woman, what have I to do with
thee." [3]

But in the ideal form, the new city cannot apply one moral
standard to man, another to woman: as the new kingdom would
end by pulling down the walls between the city of the rich
and the city of the poor, so would it end by filling the gulf that
separates the kingdom of man from the kingdom of woman.
Both are persons in their own right and the one cannot be considered a slave either to man or to man-imposed functions. A
Christian cannot dispose over woman as if she were a thing or
a commodity; she has to be wooed and won; and to give herself,
if at all, freely: love for love, need for need.

We have noted that norm—being in essence instinct transformed and ordered—is only secondarily subject to intellectualization. Hence, prior to the logical construct, we would expect to
find some signs of a new feeling existing in the relation between
man and woman. Following such a lead we are returned—not
to Mary, the Mother—but to the other Mary who "wrought a
good work upon" [4] the Founder, and who was first to greet Him
at the sunrise of Easter. For while "from time immemorial women
must have inspired men with an inclination distinct from desire
. . . romantic love has a definite date: it sprang up . . . when
some person or persons conceived the idea of absorbing love into

[3] *St. John*, II, 4.   [4] *St. Matthew*, XXVI, 10.

a kind of supernatural feeling, into religious emotion created by
Christianity and launched by the new religion into the world.
. . . It was love which began by plagiarizing mysticism, borrowing from it its fervours, its raptures, its ecstacies: in using the language of a passion it has transfigured, mysticism has only resumed
possession of its own." [5] The new emotion creates its own climate,
its own contagion, and its own code. It enriches, in widening
circles, the relation between man and woman; it starts a fermentation out of which the family emerges renewed. By following this
process we come to follow the growth of the institutional nuclei
around which a new society evolves.

The new emotional compulsion places the function of reproduction in a new context. Men and women, freed, we may suppose,
from the tyranny of lust over will, would cease to consider children as mere symbols or mere means of family survival. Children,
no less than women, would be considered as persons in their own
right. They have a right to a life of their own, and to partake
of the dignity of all human beings. They would have to come
wanted into the world; and no parents would—through prevent-
able improvidence—like to render themselves so destitute as to
give their children stones instead of bread and thus destine them
to the early graves of the poor. Parents cannot protect children
from all hazards; but they can through wise behavior reduce these
hazards. And says the apostle: "If any provide not for his own,
and especially for those of his own house, he hath denied the faith,
and is worse than an infidel." [6] St. Augustine, in his turn, says
that "in the family of the faithful man, the heavenly pilgrim,
there the commanders are indeed the servants of those they seem

[5] Bergson, *The Two Sources*, p. 34.   [6] 1 *Timothy*, v, 8.

to command: ruling not in ambition, but being bound by careful duty: not in proud sovereignty, but in nourishing pity." [7]

Aristotle taught us that training in virtue presupposed some measure of material comfort and leisure. The new city expanding the requirement of virtue from the upper kingdom to the whole of the city becomes, therefore, in one sense more "materialistic" than the old. The golden rule implies a pity that is not only universal but also "nourishing." This insistence on the close interrelation between what is spiritual and what is material has not ceased to shock the finer sensibilities of the rich. And in the defense of opponents to the new ethics, it may be said that a city— "distributing to the necessity of saints, given to hospitality" [8]— naturally exposes itself to the real danger of starving the reproductive function. Indeed, there have in all times been Christian groups which have believed in and practiced a complete suppression of this function. Though the Founder Himself may be, and has been, variously interpreted on this point, He says: "Have ye not read, that he which made them at the beginning, made them male and female . . . and they twain shall be one flesh? . . . What therefore God hath joined together, let no man put asunder." [9] Still, when the new feeling begins to stir up the city, the surplus required for the life more abundant can come only from two sources: from the possessions of the rich or from resources previously devoted to reproduction. Hence, when the Founder now claims at least part of these resources for popular consumption, it would, at first sight, appear as if he had in mind a short splurge of capital consumption to be followed by the end of the world; for obviously neither of these sources affords the basis of

---

[7] *City of God,* book xix, chap. 14.   [8] *Romans,* xii, 13.
[9] *St. Matthew,* xix, 4–6.

permanent prosperity. We are led into the field of eschatological speculation, long a favorite means of escape from the intellectual labors of serious ethics. While we are not competent to enter upon a technical discussion of this, it suffices to point out that there is no logical need for it. The Founder Himself tried in a series of parables to impress upon minds, tied down by the static concepts of the old world, the dynamic implications of the new kingdom. In the parable of the talents he blasted the "wicked and slothful servant" who failed to return his master's money with usury: "for unto every one that hath shall be given, and he shall have abundance; but from him that hath not shall be taken away even that which he hath." [10] And in view of this dynamic concept of society the new ethics—which is necessarily foolishness in terms of static thought—falls into a natural, logical sequence.

In order to understand this sequence consider the situation when the new families begin to form a first community within the old city. When it begins to limit births (by restraint in marriage, by later marriage, or by an increasing proportion of celibates) it retains—above the usual transfer to Caesar—a little surplus of its own. Following the Founder's commandment and its own feeling, it uses this surplus to raise family consumption above previously prevailing levels. Now, we have observed already in the old city a certain relationship between standard of consumption and mortality. For when consumption fell below the minimum for existence, population was reduced; when it increased, population increased. The true significance of this relationship was overshadowed by the social impossibility of reducing the birth rate; and mythmakers would be careful to hide from the multitude this potential gate to a more abundant life. But in a general way

[10] *St. Matthew,* xxv, 29.

—though long hidden from the view of reason—it has always been true that, when people are amply fed, clothed, housed, and cared for, they tend to live longer, filling more fully their allotted span of life. This relationship is most obvious in the case of children. Hence, having found a means of limiting births, the first effect of the new policy is to increase the average expectation of life in the new community. And as, in the long run, population numbers can be considered as the product of number of births per year and the average expectation of life, the fall in mortality makes it possible to maintain permanently a stable population with a smaller number of births. If the average life can be prolonged from a score to three score years (which has happened in parts of Christendom), the number of children required to keep a population stable is decreased by two thirds. The shift over from the old to the new population type (the former based on deaths, the latter on births as chief variable) releases resources previously tied up in abortive reproduction. Moreover, as the new type contains a greater proportion of persons in the productive ages, the product available per capita further increases. Hence, even disregarding such savings as may be effected by the final elimination of the function of order and defense, the new population policy tends, to a point, to pay its own way.

But the margin available for such developments is not unlimited. If families kept on trying to maximize consumption per capita, they would also go on decreasing expenditure on reproduction until this expense would be eliminated altogether. In order to create lasting balance, therefore, a further criterion of policy is needed. It is not too difficult to perceive that a stable balance, under the new assumptions, results only if (on each level of habit) popular consumption is driven just to the point of highest average expectation of life compatible with stable population. It remains to be considered how the voluntary actions of families can meet this condition.

The desire for lasting balance is implicit in the universal striving for the common good. In actuality many circumstances combine to prevent a precise balance from being reached. But there is room for trial and error, for experiment and change, as long as the balance remains self-corrective. And considering the general tendencies of a normative society, there would surely grow up institutional aids to policy: we would expect the rise of normative, but voluntarily accepted, qualifications as to the economic competency required for marriage and the rearing of children—or, in the sense of the classical economists, certain standards of living. Such standards, intelligently adapted to shifting circumstance, could prevent variations in population from straying too far from the theoretical optimum. And in actual fact, one would expect that the transition would be further eased by simultaneous changes in the efficiency of economic habit. It was not always easy, even in the old city, to prevent invention and innovation. In the new city the dynamic impulses already considered render such prevention undesirable and, for that matter, impossible. The dynamic impulses affect economic habit in several, often devious, ways.

Impressions of infancy and childhood are decisive elements of character formation. Changes in family-life, therefore, cannot help but change the character of successive generations. The new family, releasing resources for the better material care of children, supplies also a new measure of security, love, and tenderness. Children grow up in an atmosphere which is gradually cleansed from the fear of the ancient categorical imperatives. As myth is more and more replaced by norm, men are liberated from rational postulate and freed from the blinds of innate ideas. The new city creates a climate of intellectual liberty; it can afford to listen to reason, not as to a master, but as to a good servant. Freed from the cares of rule, it can consider all kind of new end-means relationships. It can give vent to curiosity, roam around the universe, and return with strange data and observations. These it can arrange in attractive patterns, check them against experience, and gradually discover ways of interpreting and predicting events. By obedience to such rules, man becomes capable of greater control over his environment. Reason supplies him with alternative ways of doing things and ends by discovering the art of making inventions. This liberation of reason creates a potentiality of higher productivity, larger surplus, and more abundant life.

But the application of potential habit is not an automatic or inevitable process. It would be childish to assume that a mere accumulation of knowledge in itself guarantees progress and good life. Change in habit is always, in a measure, the result of effort; and such change is possible only under certain objectively given conditions. For the present purpose it is sufficient to recall a few of the most important.

Plato told the citizens that God had made some men out of gold and others out of brass. The ruler should train each man— according to the native metal in him—into habits preconceived by reason. What in a man did not fit his appointed role had to be pruned, suppressed, or diverted. Plato made an enemy of appetite. But basing the social construct on appetite, or instinct, converted into norm, the new city could not forcefully impose preconceived roles on its members. It had to make a further bold assumption which only ex post facto could be put to the test of experience. The Apostle, having in mind the embryonic new city, wrote: "For as we have many members in one body, and all members have not the same office; so we being many, are one body in Christ, and every one members one of another . . . having . . . gifts differing according to the grace that is given to us. . . ."[11] In other words, the possibility of realizing the new city rests upon a potential harmony of human gifts when joined together in a local union of citizens. The releasing and inspiring force resides in the universal consciousness. And partial as experience remains, it tends to confirm the idea that the originality of man, under certain conditions, supplies freely the foundation for social growth and development. And a later founder of state repeated the belief in a future state where this originality could be given full play. He depicts a city in which "each individual [has] the opportunity to develop and exercise all his faculties, physical and mental, in all directions; in which, therefore, productive labor will become a pleasure instead of a burden,"[12] and in which consequently society would receive "from each according to his abilities" and give "to each according to his needs."

But even supposing experience to have confirmed the existence of such a potential harmony of gifts, society could only profit from it if society has the means of their development. There is required a general system of education, adjusted to each stage of development; there is need for liberty of choice and, above all, the means and the leisure necessary for study and training in new skills. And as the development of surplus depends upon the previous development of skills, so does the development of skills depend upon previous surplus. Thus the question of education comes largely to turn about the availability of surplus, and the courage and vision to risk it wisely in undertakings which offer no tangible or im-

[11] *Romans,* XII, 4–6.   [12] *Anti-Dühring,* p. 322.

mediate return. And many habits desirable in themselves cannot be applied unless previous surplus is available for investment in necessary tools and equipment. Moreover, many forms of investment are impracticable unless the habit system as a whole has already reached a certain perfection and degree of integration.

Hence, for a number of reasons, the question of surplus becomes even more vital in the dynamic setting of the new city than it was in the static construction of the old. It is hardly necessary to remind ourselves again how pitifully small this surplus has been, and still is, in most parts of the world. And the smaller the relative surplus, the greater is the sacrifice required to scrape together new savings. In the new city such sacrifice cannot be imposed from above, nor with the harsh methods employed by a ruthless ruler. It has to be voluntary and made by the families themselves. To the new man, thrift and soberness are implicit in his responsibility for his own and for the whole. But it is difficult, if not impossible, for servants, slaves, and day-laborers to find the means and opportunities of saving and investment. It comes more naturally to independent farmers, artisans, craftsmen, and persons engaged in trade. The citizens of the new movement, it may be expected, will tend to be attracted by such occupations as offer to the individual possibilities of independent action. And in Christendom such occupations have, in fact, become the economic nuclei of new order. But out of the free activities of families— and the innumerable forms of voluntary association created by them—have come the surplus and the initiative which, in spite of the tragic failures and betrayals, have let Christendom create a civilization more dynamic and more highly integrated and perhaps more kindly than any of which we have the record.

The progress of the new city resolves itself in a series of interconnected events. We have some experience which permits us to conceive of its beginnings, and the condition of continuous balance. We have no means of exhausting the potentiality still resting in it. But partial as experience may be, it joins with theory in declaring that the sequence of events now studied is the result of effort, and that it is reversible. The dynamism of the new city rests in the last instance in the character of its citizens, in their obedience to norm, and to the education and training they receive in the family and its instrumentalities. And anything that in any way tends to slow up, stop, or reverse the new process of character-formation, slows up, stops, or reverses the process of social growth. And so doing it calls forth the need for external controls, and with it a return to the ways and means of the old city of reason. No technical device can, in a free society, serve as a substitute for character. In the last instance, the most precious gift of the new city rests in the primacy of the inner kingdom: for so far as social analysis has yet penetrated, it confirms that in seeking "first the kingdom of God, and his righteousness" then, and then only are "all . . . things . . . added unto you." [13]

[13] *St. Matthew*, VI, 33.

18

A CITY
Laying the Monsters

YE HAVE HEARD THAT IT HATH BEEN SAID, THOU
SHALT LOVE THY NEIGHBOR, AND HATE THINE
ENEMY: BUT I SAY UNTO YOU, LOVE YOUR ENE-
MIES, BLESS THEM THAT CURSE YOU, DO GOOD
TO THEM THAT HATE YOU, AND PRAY FOR THEM
WHICH DESPITEFULLY USE YOU, AND PERSECUTE
YOU.[1]

THE NEW CITY comes with a feeling of urgency: it likens itself to
a ship perilously voyaging through time, or to pilgrims pressing
on towards their true country. A sense of direction is there, but
the final destination has remained and should remain a distant
vision. It is not surprising that this is so, for, if the new city
represents what finally amounts to a process of change, the ordinary mind would be unable to visualize it except in images
borrowed from the static and blurred by the vibration of new
energy. Whether or not philosophy and theology have been successful in dealing with states of pure change, social theory has been
unable to dispense with points of reference in the static. Hence,
social growth has, as we have said, for purposes of analysis, to
be conceived as an interplay between two systems—an interplay

[1] *St. Matthew,* v, 43, 44.

which naturally forms itself into a sample model of a historical process.

Let us put again "the pattern shewed to [us] on the mount" [2] in relation to the model of the static city. To start with, the new pattern existed only as a potentiality in a single soul; but this potentiality was universal both in scope and ambition. The Stranger came as a conqueror and took the risks of one: unless He had the means of "binding the strong man" who was in residence, He had better retire to the Stoic tower of contemplation. And as He lacked outer power and dwelt in the multitude, His penetration had already for these reasons to be directed towards the inner kingdom: He had to plant nuclei of new order in the existing city. But the risk of physical extermination of a new movement is very real, particularly in the beginning. If the guardians of existing order should become aware of the potential danger these nuclei represent, they would stamp them out. The chief priests would perhaps be the first to sense the danger implied in the new teachings: in tracking down and silencing the agitators they would only follow the bidding of duty and interest as they must conceive it. The Founder, teaching in parables, was wise in playing down the political consequences that are implicit in His system as in all other systems of ethics or theology purporting to affect and direct human events. The parables gave up their secrets to the few possessing the key; but they remained closed to the many who had it not, and particularly to those who were trained to think in terms of outer power. When the experts on morals pointed out the political implications of the new teachings, Pilate reacted as one uncertain of his own mind: "When Pilate therefore heard that saying, he was the more afraid; and went again into the

[2] *Hebrews*, VIII, 5.

judgment hall, and saith unto Jesus, Whence art thou? But Jesus gave him no answer." [3] Pilate was at length intimidated and put the Founder to death, but he let the disciples go their way unmolested: the all-important nuclei of the new city were thus spared. During the period of germination, Christianity was well served by its seeming political indifference, by its teachings couched in parables, and by the protective silences of its leaders.

The surviving and spreading nuclei of Christendom had to exist in the outer kingdoms of the old city: "wherefore the necessaries of this life are common, both to the faithful and the infidel, and to both their families." [4] The concept of two inner kingdoms, abiding together in a common outer kingdom, has often been confusing; but it is only by understanding this relationship that we can rationally analyze the policy of the new city. It is true that a community of Christians would render the old order obsolete, for social balance is implicit in a universal realization of the pattern of the Mount; but prior to the realization of this ideal the new man depends as much as the old upon the order of the old city for his daily sustenance: the old order is preferable to no order, or to the cataclysm of interregnum. It is in the common interest of the just and the unjust that order, such as it is, should function smoothly and cheaply, and it would frustrate the new city if the old should be completely dissolved before the universal realization of the new inner kingdom.

But the city now has double projection systems: old myth and new norm. We know how vulnerable myth is to such disturbance; it would be fairly easy to provoke interregnum; or rather, positive intervention is required to prevent it. This is why the new man

[3] *St. John,* XIX, 8, 9.
[4] St. Augustine, *City of God,* book XIX, chap. 17.

should, during an indeterminate period of transition, "willingly obey such laws of the temporal city as order things pertaining to the sustenance of this mortal life, to the end that both cities might observe a peace in such things as are pertinent hereunto." Indeed the new man even uses the old order "for the attainment of the peace celestial . . . because being a citizen, he must not be all for himself, but be sociable in his life and action." [5] The faithful man becomes concerned both with the outer and inner kingdoms and he "may not be so given to contemplation that he neglect the good of his neighbor, nor so far in love with action that he forget divine speculation." [6] It is really in his own interest, then, that the new man concedes to Caesar such powers as are needed for maintenance of outer order; this concession cannot be traced back to ancient obligation or belief: it is a necessary condition for the speeding of the coming of new order. In the old city myth seemed to procure the voluntary assent required to prevent the escape of the monsters. But by obeying the ruler voluntarily—for the sake of the new city—the new man is already, by his citizenship in the new inner kingdom, in a state of voluntary assent to the old outer order. If the ruler and his advisers only perceived it, they have ceased to need myth in dealing with the citizens of the new city. This opens up a new perspective to rule: for in fact, the new citizen has already granted more to Caesar than the old, limited by self-consciousness, was ever able to do.

Then, anticipating, as it were, the voluntary assent that myth (though more imperfectly) was designed to procure, the new man cannot, in the nature of things, remain the subject of myth. Indeed, submitting to it, he would by removing the true basis of voluntary assent, decrease the assent that the submission was de-

signed to promote. It is, therefore, in the true interest of Caesar
to leave the nuclei of the new city in peace. But when the new city
refuses Caesar's authority over the inner kingdom, it is principally
for another reason. Caesar, brought up in static conceptions of
things and burdened by the cares of rule, could not help trying
to convert norm into myth and thus stunting the growth of the
city by bringing it into the sphere of the static and subordinating
the inner kingdom to the outer. Hence, the new man can remain
what he is only by being the subject solely of God: Caesar's rights
end at the point where God's begin, or rather all rights belong
to God and Caesar's are to be understood as concessions. "Hence
came it that the two hierarchies could not be combined in one
religion, but must needs dissent herein, so that the good part was
fain to bear the pride and persecution of the bad, had not their
own multitude sometimes and the providence of God continu-
ally stood for their protection." [7]

The fathers would say that the need for outer submission was
"caused" by "sin" and that it would disappear only with the victory of the new city. In another sense, we say that this submission
serves as a barrier against a sudden and unlimited (and thus
socially dissolving) dynamism; it is a barrier against the potential
anarchy of undisciplined norm. But important as these considerations may be, they have not laid bare the most subtle of the
mechanisms now brought into being. And as these final issues
become more easy to understand at a later stage of the growth
of the new city, let it be imagined that it has come to knit together a whole network of nuclei covering, directly and indirectly,
the whole of the lower kingdom. It would seem natural if the
masses were now to rise, sweep away the upper kingdoms, destroy

[7] *Ibid.,* book XIX, chap. 17.

old institutions, and found the kingdom of God with the aid of the sword. Weighty reasons and glittering promises would not be wanting.

To deal with this great temptation let us recall some familiar relationships. When self-consciousness heralded the rise of the city out of nature, we encountered the conflict between private and social interest: myth arose as the conciliator between them. But a perfect inner balance, permitting obligation and belief to appear as one, was an ideal construct, unlikely to be reached in reality. Hence in order to protect order against residual conflict (i.e., private resistance to rule) there was need for a compulsion which was supplied by the physical arm of order. Fear induced men to submit to the ruling will, and in this sense fear became the ultimate binding force of the old city. But this solution carried its own penalty. Frustration of private impulse created the monsters and the need for more force to keep them down, and so on. The need of force in government is therefore a sign of imperfection in the social system; and the prevention of interregnal explosions of violence became a lasting but unsolved problem of legitimate government. It is somewhat naive then to believe that, because force may be needed in government, it is either in itself desirable or a sufficient condition thereof.

Consider now these relationships in connection with social growth. Expenditure of force by government creates fears; these fears are mutual to ruler and ruled, and become boundless unless checked by myth. But fear, in the last analysis, represents the force of love inverted. Hence, as expressions of one and the same primary energy, fear and love become mutually exclusive: as love casteth out fear, fear casteth out love. Any policy, therefore, which tends to increase fear also tends to decrease the availability of love

as a socially active force; it freezes the energies which create and
maintain society and drains the process of norm-formation of its
driving impulse. Hence, any process of social violence, whatever
its origin and justification, is contrary to the true interest of the
new movement. Fear, by suppressing norm, leaves the city swept
and garnished for the return of myth. For men preferring "any
sort of peace and safety even to freedom" [8] seek, prodded by
reason, their security in the planned authority of the static and
the mythical. Even a well-intentioned and privately noble wielder
of the sword cannot avoid the consequences of his own action.
Having released fear, and thus prevented the flow of love, he becomes dependent upon fear; as a ruler he returns society to the
forms from which he pretended to save it. But as his activity also
would tend to destroy residual systems of myth which, whatever
their shortcomings, to some extent mitigated the severity of previous rule, his dependence on force and fear would become total.
This explains the close historical correlation between the "good
intentions" of a new ruler and the severity of the terror which he
must employ in support of rule; "good" rulers of this sort are,
almost without exception, more dangerous and bloodthirsty than
the "bad" rulers of established tradition. It is therefore the nature
of the process of social growth (which process should not be confused with the pretended dynamism of men who are in reality
returning the city to a static form) that prevents the new man
from having recourse to violence. The prohibition of the use of
force is so far from being caused by fear that actually it rests
upon the necessity of conquering fear. The policy of nonviolence
is the opposite of passivity: it is a condition for active life and
growth. In order to understand better what still may appear as

[8] *Ibid.,* book XVIII, chap. 2.

a paradox, it is good to mount the observation post of the traditional ruler.

This man needs to command such blind obedience as would be the fruit of voluntary assent to his will: the chances of survival, and the pleasures of rule, are greatest when voluntary assent can be had free and without effort. Myth purported to secure such assent, but the residual need of force in government showed the limitations of reason. Moreover, the constant outward veneration that had to be accorded to myth circumscribed the ruler's liberty of action in the state: so did his constant need to be on his guard against the monsters. The terror that the ruler had to instill among his subjects—and even more his attempts to police their thoughts—were measures of his own fears of them. But in this game of mutual fears, it was the ruled who had to pay first and most dearly. It is natural (and hard to censor) for subjects to respond to cruelty and oppression with hate; but it is not wise. Hate generates more fear in the ruler, who projects his fears back on the ruled in the form of more terror, and so on. And the ruler continues to have the upper hand as long as organized society lasts. The multitude can escape the consequence only by removing the cause which is (in part) their own hate. The ruler's fears, and thus the terror, can be limited and decreased only when the multitude raises itself to the level of universal consciousness where it can overcome the reaction of a natural man to those who despitefully use and persecute him. It can be added that the people would gain nothing by destroying a particular ruler: the new one would be faced with the same necessity as the first and react, if he wants to survive, in much the same way.

The absolute ruler is ever suspicious of conspiracy and frowns upon any voluntary association among subjects. When he discovers that the new city has its own leaders, habits, norms, and even transfer, he reacts according to tradition. And his ire becomes more inflamed when he is told by priests and philosophers that the new community refuses to recognize his supremacy over the inner kingdom. Suppression may appear a wise and necessary policy; but in the absence of resistance, and particularly in view of the folly of destroying a great part of that multitude which forms the strength of rule, such attempts can hardly be prolonged or wholehearted. And to tell the truth, Caesar was rarely in love with the divine role. He played it in order to acquire the necessary means of outer rule and it was more of an embarrassment to him than a pleasure. And as "the counsels of princes are more frequently influenced by views of temporal advantage than by considerations of abstract and speculative truth," [9] it is almost overwhelmingly probable that if a ruler could find a cheaper and less bothersome way of producing voluntary assent he would in the course of time follow it. Mere consistency would not forever block the road of self-interest. Such a conversion of a ruler does not need to follow some simple scheme: it can be varied. But consider here, by way of illustration, Gibbon's description of the reasons which led to the adoption of Christianity by the Roman emperors.

"Every principle which had once maintained the vigour and purity of Rome and Sparta was long since extinguished. . . . Under these discouraging circumstances a prudent magistrate might observe with pleasure the progress of a religion which diffused among the people a . . . universal system of ethics [so constructed] that the magistrates might sheath the sword of justice among a people . . . actuated by . . . universal love. The pas-

[9] Gibbon, *The Decline and Fall of the Roman Empire* (The Modern Library), vol. I, p. 639.

sive and unresisting obedience which bows under the yoke of authority, or even oppression, must have appeared in the eyes of an absolute monarch the most conspicuous and useful of the evangelic virtues. . . . The humble Christians were sent into the world as sheep among wolves; and since they were not permitted to employ force even in defense of their religion, they should be still more criminal if they were tempted to shed the blood of their fellow-creatures in disputing the vain privileges . . . of this transitory life. . . . [A prudent magistrate] might add that the throne of the emperors would be established on a fixed and permanent basis if all their subjects, embracing the Christian doctrine, should learn to suffer and to obey." [10]

The deep troubles of the universal ruler were due to the evaporation of myth; and when in the end he becomes impotent to stave off the unrolling interregnum, he would be a strange man if he did not try to utilize such integrating force as might yet be available. And if it should be found nowhere but in the new city, he would, in the interest of survival, have to approach it. The private character of the ruler would not be of great relevance, for, if he is rational, the voluntary submission of subjects would needs appear to him as the pearl of great price. In order to buy it he would be right in giving up beliefs, habits, and pretenses which had ceased to be useful except to the priestly class to which they afforded occasion for power and wealth. Hence, by refusing to engage "the strong man" on his own ground and with his own weapons, and by administering to his true need rather than harming him, the new city has created a situation where the ruler must seek its aid. It is the ruler who now must ask for a *modus vivendi*. The processes leading up to this climacteric moment are simple

[10] *Ibid.*, vol. I, pp. 639–641.

and obvious; but even the ex post facto analysis retains some of the sharpness of the paradoxical. It is difficult to describe the quality of mind required for the anticipation of this experience, or the boldness needed to act upon it.

Try to visualize this encounter between the cities. On the one hand we have proud and violent rulers vested with every divine attribute, on the other, the subject multitudes. A kingdom of shadows, they appear. There is a movement in the mass, a new way of life, a state of mind rather than an organization. The movement is centered around a principle, and its confessed ruler is God. It is an elusive but real system of power; and lacking institutional equipment it cannot be reached by formal negotiation or snared by treaties. Hence, to come to grips with such a formless but real system of power there is no way but joining it. Caesar must confess himself a Christian. He has to enter the fold in sheep's clothing, but has he also changed his wolf's nature?

Historians are fond of repeating anecdotes which are said to throw light on the private characters of rulers and to classify them in the categories of good or bad. But a ruler, in order to remain a ruler, is in the end guided, not by private tastes and preferences, but by objective necessities. Even if Caesar, now entering into the fold, is of most excellent piety, he cannot endure unless he remains first and last a ruler. Joining a movement—whose martyrs have not yet returned unto dust—he does so fundamentally for selfish reasons; and it is not unlikely that the sheep remain in danger. But future danger is no measure of a triumph won. At this moment the lion appears to lie down with the lamb; and there need be no doubt that we are moving into a spiritual and political climate of a new kind. The policy of nonviolence has moved from the land of the potential and is reaching the charted shore of experience. Nothing should mar the serenity of the faithful's *Te Deum*.

The road ahead may be full of danger, error, and betrayal. But the two cities have become so intimately interconnected that, without an understanding of the laws of each and the laws which govern their interrelationships, we cannot hope to analyze the historical process as it has proceeded, and is proceeding, in the West. We have yet to acquire the tools and skills necessary for this task: at this point, therefore, we must end the examination of the general principles which are proper to the ideal model. It would be another task to lay bare that tension, between the two cities that constitutes the inner drama of Christendom. The period during which the new city was formed in the multitude is covered by a kind of amnesia, and in order to understand it there is need for a special kind of theoretical analysis. From now on the drama moves onto the better-lighted stage of history. There arise in the outer kingdoms new vital institutions purporting to represent the new city or to regulate the relation between the cities. We refer more specially to the churches which seem to become mechanisms of compromise between the static and the dynamic, myth and norm, violence and nonviolence.

The new city represents a social process or, if we like, a method of change. It is, in the old sense, no city at all, and in the new sense "a city without end." Hence, whatever the churches and states of the new city may like to pretend, they become, at the best, intellectually confused if they identify themselves, or any other temporal institution, with the kingdom of God. This pilgrim city represents power that makes it possible for actual cities to move towards more abundant life: it puts its imprint on social reality. But no sooner have actual kingdoms reached one station, than the city of God, moved by continuous norm-formation, has leapt to a new position. To foresee the final destination would be to have that preknowledge of potential experience which, so far, has been reserved for God.

We found a method of structural change to be prerequisite for social survival; we have found now that nonviolence is a condition necessary for such change. There is resolved another apparent paradox which the Founder placed as a guidepost on the road to the more abundant life:

"Blessed are the meek: for they shall inherit the earth." [11]

[11] *St. Matthew*, v, 5.

19

A CITY

For the Making of Gods

THEIRS IS THE RESPONSIBILITY, THEN, FOR DECIDING
IF THEY WANT MERELY TO LIVE, OR INTEND TO
MAKE JUST THE EXTRA EFFORT REQUIRED FOR FUL-
FILLING, EVEN ON THIS REFRACTORY PLANET,
THE ESSENTIAL FUNCTION OF THE UNIVERSE,
WHICH IS A MACHINE FOR THE MAKING OF GODS.

—*Bergson* [1]

IN LATE PERIODS OF DISBELIEF and enlightenment it is common for
men to fancy that they have severed relations with the gods. But
if all men are conditioned by their civilization, they are what
they are partly because of the gods without whom civilizations
could not have arisen. Indirectly men remain debtors of gods, and
it is a wise man that guards against the defense-mechanism which
is said to be characteristic of a debtor. The more rational men
profess themselves to be, the more should they beware of the
common error of censoring their data. That cities "consist of gods
and men" is a fact open to easy historical verification. Gods,
therefore, cannot avoid becoming data of universal relevance to
theory. Whether or not gods "really" exist, or have existed, is a
subject irrelevant to social theory, whatever may be said of its

[1] *The Two Sources of Morality and Religion*, p. 306.

relevance to metaphysics. Gods are social entities recognizable by
means of the agreed-upon divine attributes and the worship accorded to them by the faithful. The social theorist—as opposed to
the propagandist—cannot afford to adopt, or to be influenced by,
the attitudes towards the gods prevailing at different times and
places among different groups of men: such attitudes are themselves data relevant to theory, and as such to be dispassionately
studied and, if possible, explained. But if it was difficult to deal
with gods presumably dead, it is difficult indeed to deal truly, and
without presumption, with the living God of one's own tradition.

Plato assumed a "revolution in the soul" in rulers and guardians
so as to provide the type of man corresponding to the needs of the
Republic. The natural man had to be taught how to silence the
clamor of passion and how to listen to the voice of social reason.
Plato tried to remove from his city everything that would help or
strengthen passion in its conflict with reason. He feared, in particular, men's natural inclination to imitate those men or those
mythical heroes whom they liked and admired: for, "Did you
never observe how imitations, beginning in early youth and continuing far into life, at length grow into habits and become second
nature, affecting body, voice, and mind?" [2] If the emotions are
thus permitted to attach themselves to nonrational entities, character formation would escape the severe tutelage of reason. But
in a city which first spoke with the tongue of emotion, the attitude towards reason and thus towards imitation would change.
For in order to create a primary order amongst loves it is obviously necessary first to appeal to emotion; but this appeal must
not be haphazard or arbitrary for, as Plato knew, this other
necessity "which lovers know" is subject to its own law. In order

[2] *Republic,* 395d.

to create a new social type and "straighten out the emotions" we have to speak a language understood by the emotions and avoid the primary complications of cerebration. Not only does this order of events hold true subjectively, but it becomes particularly vital for a movement which, unlike Stoicism, has to work its way upwards from the depths of society; the new city was from the outset concerned with the poor in spirit, the publicans, and the harlots rather than with the well born, the wise, and the rich.

The universal language of love (being at bottom primary energy) is life; it is only when love presents itself in the form of life that it directly appeals to the emotions of the multitude of men. Few, perhaps, would be bold enough to affirm that they had begun to grasp the full intellectual implications of the words on the Mount; but fewer still, we believe, could truthfully affirm that they had never felt—even as an echo—the impact of a life lived according to that pattern. Men do not tire of "services rendered"; and the warmth of a life of Charity attracts emotion and tends, by its own power, to set itself up as a model of imitation. Hence, if this be so, the realization in fact of the new city turns around the all-important problem of character-formation, which in particular raises the question of how to find and render operative a universal, central model of imitation. We have, no doubt, observed character-formation through imitation on the small secondary scale; but the formation of the first, primary model offers problems which are strange to common experience, or rather must lie altogether outside of it. Men are taught to take their gods for granted, and in order to achieve perspective let us return for a moment to the meeting point of myth and norm.

Myths must be visualized as projected from a point in the past, representing one given position of balanced habit. Norms must be visualized as projected from a point in the future, representing an imagined position of balanced habit. Myth tends to freeze a given pattern of social events; norm to dissolve such a pattern and to impose a new one. When the projection point of norm was fixed (i.e., represented by any ideal city of reason), the moving social plane would sooner or later (in a successful social mutation) pass the norm projection point, which thenceforward must be considered indistinguishable from a myth projection point: norm, from there on, assumes the nature and function of myth and becomes identical with it. These are briefly the sequences which subjected the old city to the recurring "challenge" and "response" mechanisms, and the cumulating risks of a series of social mutations and interregna.

Hence, we deduced that in an organic process of growth the fixed norm-projection point (i.e., any a priori social construct) had to be replaced by a constantly receding one (i.e., a principle of norm-formation). The formulation of "ends" had to become an integral part of the social process itself inseparable from "means": one apparent set of "end-means relationships" being organically followed by a more distant relationship, and so on. The norm-formation point of the new city can only be thought to reside in love of the whole, or a universal consciousness. Hence, as integration implies friction, and pure dynamism nonentity, a moving social plane could approach but never reach this final projection point. Or turn the argument around: as full realization of the ideal of love would liquefy all forms as we are able to conceive them, it would lead also to the destruction of society as we are at present able to conceive it. Such a possibility must appear to us as infinitely distant and without actuality. It is nevertheless present, and intellectually accounted for, in that final state of being in which, according to the apostle, God becomes "all in all"; all present form bursts, and reintegrates into a "new heaven" and a "new earth."

We have seen then that the norm-formation point must in theory be an infinite distance (or what amounts to the same, constantly receding) from the social plane. We have seen also that the normative demands of the new city, to become operative, must be translated into the terms of a compelling model of imitation. More simply, the transcendent and infinitely distant final norm-formation point must be duplicated by, or become immanent in, a corresponding model of imitation present in and appealing to the city. It is obvious, therefore, that the requirements which this final model of imitation meets are of a peculiar nature, and different from all that men had previously conceived. Unless the translation of the principle of norm-formation into a pattern of imitation shall give rise to the static or the quasi-dynamic, the final model of imitation must embody nothing else than the full potentiality of the norm-forming principle. It is obliged, in pushing the dynamic to the absolute, to go beyond what is possible for any society or any natural man as such. In the familiar terms, the model of imitation must be identical to the divine love that creates the universe and without which nothing was "made that was made." [3] And this is why the new kingdom could not come into operation unless the "Word [that] was God . . . was made flesh, and dwelt among us." [4]

The concept of God is the measure of man and civilization; the discovery that "God is love" enlarges the measure of both. But we have discovered too that this incredible leap forward required the apparently impossible of man: indeed it created the need for

[3] *St. John*, 1, 3.   [4] *St. John*, 1, 1, 14.

the superhuman effort of divine incarnation. Consider Plato. He could soar like an eagle above the Republic: his soul could seek refuge in the "sacred everlasting calm" of the ideal. In virtue of his superior vision he had not only the ability, but the duty, to lead his fellowmen by means of the necessary lie. But Jesus had to descend into the dark cave of the world. He had to become one with the prisoners; and, supplying an alternative to the necessary lie, He could afford to release the liberating truth; but this alternative meant that He had also to become one with the new kingdom: His ways its ways, His truth its truth, and His life its life. While man, He had to become the first-born of God.

The prisoners in the cave could not be free agents. Self, with the insistence of natural law, led them to try to save their lives; they thus had no way of overcoming fear—the reverse aspect of love centered on self. And so necessary was self-love to the old city that it had added the talismans of fear to its heraldry: the fasces, the sword, the many-headed monsters, and the dark cross itself. And as long as these talismans retained the power to provoke fear, so long did they divert the flow of love needed for the birth and growth of the new city. Hence, a new pattern of imitation could become operative only by removing this centering of love upon self, the primary cause of the power of the city's talismans. The first movement of the center of love from self to God and through Him back to the whole was achieved in the mystic experience and the simultaneous social emergence of a universal consciousness. This inner experience of chosen spirit now seeks a form fitted to the social drama in a seamless pattern of imitation.

Jesus, then, had knowingly to let Himself be swept forward by the full flood of love beyond shores where human life had been possible. Man, no more than society, can support love unleashed and live. The terrific energy of a pure dynamism burns away the last fears and hesitations binding man to the static or to any of the known forms of life. Jesus cuts the umbilical cord that joins man to the old order; a Son of Man rises above the fear of death, the shadow of self. He gives His life freely, and the ruler has lost the power to take it from Him. The old talismans of fear pale away. On the road from Bethlehem to Golgotha the universal consciousness finds the model of imitation. And as the Son of Man rises to become the Son of God, there comes integration out of disintegration, or in the apostle's words, incorruption out of corruption. This is the climacteric crisis of mankind. The cross becomes henceforth the talisman of hope and the sign of man's freedom. During many ages reason has been busy trying to unravel the plot of the divine comedy. But before the crucified Lord it pauses with the Angelic Doctor; his universal mind found what reason says "was no more than straw." Out of his final silent year there came, it has been said, the lasting words of adoration:

> Devoutly I adore thee, hidden God,
> Behind these forms in very truth concealed.
> To thee my heart entirely yields itself,
> Utterly rapt in contemplating thee.
>
> .   .   .
>
> I do believe each word God's Son has said:
> There is no word of truth more true than this.
> Divinity alone the cross concealed,
> But here his manhood likewise is concealed.
>
> .   .   .
>
> O Jesus, whom I glimpse behind the veil,
> Grant me, I pray, the grace for which I thirst:

> Let me behold thy face without that veil
> And in the glory of thy sight be blessed.[5]

Reason withdrawn into a great creative emotion follows the universal pattern of return and encounters the world with sleep-refreshed eyes: experience is reborn. Reason had conceived the need for new order but was impotent to give it birth. Meanwhile, man has become God acting on the social stage; by the light of Easter, reason can watch the growth of new civilization. Theory had pointed to the need for a pattern of imitation; analysis was capable of giving it the necessary outlines. But it is for experience (and not for *ex ante* authority) to find out how this suddenly incarnated pattern has impressed itself upon reality. This is the master theme that would carry us beyond the ideal model. Here it suffices to point to general principles.

We observed that genius had a kind of contagious power. It can be observed that a similar power—but so supercharged as almost to be different in kind—is possessed by our Lord's life. Men,

[5]
> Adoro te devote, latens Deitas,
> Quae sub his figuris vere latitas,
> Tibi se cor meum totum subjicit,
> Quia te contemplans totum deficit.
>
> .   .   .
>
> Credo quidquid dixit Dei Filius:
> Nil hoc verbo veritatis verius.
> In cruce latebat sola Deitas:
> At hic latet simul et humanitas.
>
> .   .   .
>
> Jesu, quem velatum nunc aspicio,
> Oro, fiat illud quod tam sitio:
> Ut, te revelata cernens facie,
> Visu sim beatus tuae gloriae.

Dom A. Wilmart, *Auteurs Spirituels et textes dévots du moyen age latin* (Paris, 1932), pp. 384-385.

it appears, are endowed with degrees of moral sensibilities; some such observation would, at any rate, justify the theological constructs of grace and election. When some persons of great moral awareness are exposed to the Lord's example, they become stirred to the depths of their being. The shock experienced is not that of exhortation; it affects, as it were, the release, or birth, of preëxisting, hitherto hidden nature. For, "the longing to resemble, which ideally generates form, is an incipient resemblance; the word which we shall make our own is the word whose echo we have heard within ourselves." [6] The saintly natures and the often "obscure heroes of moral life" follow the Lord as if they "were joining an army of conquerors"; they are the medium and the avantguard of that "enthusiasm which spreads from soul to soul, unceasingly, like a conflagration." These elite form the kernels of the nuclei which the new city breathes into life. Formed into a natural pattern by the catalytic power of our Lord's life, they represent secondary sources of inspiration. Allowing for the difference between the static (or quasi-dynamic) and the dynamic, the saints correspond to the "truly virtuous man" in the philosopher's construction. Both, in existing cities, are full members of the inner kingdom of a perfect, as yet visionary, city of the future. And there is a gulf between such men and the multitude.

The history of social growth is a history of elites. Their nature and function remain hidden to an analysis applying the criteria of individual psychology. In terms of what appears in any existing society as "normal" or "healthy" the saints appear of unsound mind, in need of the care of experts who know how to cure souls. But in terms of social analysis, and in terms of the saints' own mission of changing society, maladjustment to existing habit is to

[6] Bergson, *The Two Sources of Morality and Religion*, p. 27.

them a *conditio sine qua non*. Like the genius, the saint is indif-
ferent to ruling opinion. Outer maladjustment is the paradoxical
price paid for the peace of inner fulfillment. The saint cannot
meaningfully be judged by a scale of static values.

The Lord saw the multitude with compassion. He gave particular care to the establishment of the Community of Saints serving
it. But misunderstanding comes from disregard of the functional
distance between the two. The saints are likened unto the salt of
the earth, or the leaven of the dough: it would be naive to pretend that a majority could perform their special functions. No
society can persist wholly fluid and wholly dynamic. Harmonious
social growth requires a measured liberation of a force which, because vital, can become mortal. To arrive at an ordered process
of growth, there is required insight into the social process and the
means of releasing and moderating the force needed to change
habit within limits consistent with a continuous social life. "The
Kingdom of God," says the Apostle, "is not in word, but in
power." [7] And as the social impact of this power can be considered as the product of mass and energy, the smaller the mass
of the new city the greater is the energy needed for its purpose.
The maximum need of energy is required when the new city is
still potentiality in a single soul. This maximum is achieved when
the whole of a man's primary energy—without any waste of fear
—is directed into social channels. This maximum involves a pure
manifestation of the universal consciousness, and those in whose
power it lies become the Sons of God.

Now it seems to be in the nature of things (disregarding the possibility of some violent chain-reaction) that the energy-impulse
released in the original model should spend itself as it expands.

[7] I *Corinthians*, IV, 20.

The saints form, as it were, secondary nuclei of a somewhat lower tension and so on in expanding circles. It is for the saints, *in imitatione Christi,* to affect habit around them, create new cells, which go on dividing themselves. They assume moral leadership through the power of service; and though the multitude, at times, reacts with violence, it tends in the long run to adore the martyrs and follow the saintly lead in the same way as patients follow a good physician.

As the dynamic impulse expands and exhausts itself, it modifies habit and corresponding beliefs. Society is moved forward in directions implicit in the principle of norm-formation. In the course of time it would then tend to reach a static equilibrium on a new level of integration, an equilibrium protected by the great conservation mechanisms and subject to the tendency of disintegration peculiar to the static. In effect, in a first approximation, the chief danger to Christian life would appear almost directly proportionate to the outer success, the consequent degree of institutionalization and dogmatic rationalization. The pilgrim city may come to lose the sense of its own destiny, identify itself with existing forms, protect them by controlling the means of private salvation, and look askance at the hard saying: "Except a corn of wheat fall into the ground and die, it abideth alone: but if it die, it bringeth forth much fruit." [8]

But in the end the chief danger does not rest so much in the wearing away of one wave of movement as in the absence of succeeding waves. And the separateness of the Community of Saints is perhaps most easy to understand, if we consider it as a dynamic center intended to assure a series of graded impulses of forward movement. This community is composed of souls who in a special

[8] *St. John,* XII, 24.

sense are kindled by the divine flame and strive to become perfect in love. The words of the Mount—so plainly inapplicable to the multitude of a city as a whole—become to the saints the expression of heart's desire. They are not commands as much as measures of the distance that separates the soul from God. And in this tension of new souls striving to identify themselves with the chosen model, there emerge, at times, men godlike enough to supply the impulse for a new wave of progress.

Social analysis has to accept the necessary social sequences of fermentation, movement, consolidation, and stagnation; and it is in the possibility of repetition of such sequences that theory finds a reasonable hope for progress and gradual perfection. But, though the process is possible, it is not inevitable. We face the necessity of studying the interrelationship of the two cities, where we may hope to come closer to the essence of the West; meanwhile there remains Christendom's grave danger: that of considering churches, states, and even civilizations, not as expendable means, but as ends in themselves. The saints are incorruptible witnesses testifying to our Saviour's words: "For whosoever will save his life shall lose it: and whosoever will lose his life for my sake shall find it." [9]

[9] *St. Matthew*, xvi, 25.

INDEX

INDEX

Abilities, human: potential harmony of, 217

Abortion, 50

Aeschylus, *Prometheus Vinctus,* excerpt, 92

After life, reward or punishment, 24, 26

Agriculture, effect upon location of cities, 71

Alliances, 113

Anarchy, 34, 94; sacrifice to save city from, 103; complete liberty would throw society into, 187

Anti-Dühring (Marx), excerpt, 194

Apology (Plato), excerpt, 83, 103

Apuleius, quoted, 170

Aristotle, *Politics,* excerpts, 29, 30, 46, 50, 55, 119; *Nicomachean Ethics,* excerpt, 42, 45 f., 47, 86, 89, 90; alternative for weakness in Platonic construction, 43; political philosophy, 45; concept of virtue, 45 ff.; city of, 64; problem encountered in determination of virtue, 89; quoted, 155; concept of virtue, 161, 187

Armament, *see* Defense

Art, patrons of, 139

Artisans, 7

Athanasius, St., *Contra Gentes,* excerpts, 132, 136

Attraction, world-city governed by universal power of, 172

Augustine, St., *City of God,* excerpt, 157, 175, 177, 192, 201-4 *passim*

Auteurs Spirituels . . . (Wilmart), excerpt, 240*n*; translation, 239 f.

Auxiliaries, 7

Balance, social, 29 ff., 146, 147; maintenance of, presupposes existence of order, 4; entrusted to perfect ruler, 46; when most secure, 52, 56, 57; transfer determines outer, of city, 42; guarded by myth, 54, 87; in nature of a dynamic equilibrium, 72; recreation of new, required, 87; incorporating myth and norm into a system which permits of, 88; of power, 114 f.; perfect inner, 148, 225; war reestablishes, 149; requires change in supporting system of myth, 158; in order to combine social change with, 195; enduring, established, 209; desire for lasting, 215

Barbarism, return to, 113

Behavior, human, 31; the effects and the causes of wars, 117

Belief, the supreme duty, 25; the inner kingdom (*q.v.*), 56; myth-supporting, 93, 160; disturbance in habit opposed by, 93; process which can dissolve system of, 95; areas of disagreement between obligation and, 96; conceived as a constant force, 96; interregnum required to re-create, 98;